TRUTH

THE BASICS

Truth: The Basics is a concise and engaging introduction to philosophical theories about the nature of truth. The two authors – leading philosophers in this field – build the book around a single question: what, if anything, is common to all truths, which makes them true? The book explores five important answers ('theories') to the given question: correspondence, semantic, verifiability, transparency, and plurality. For each given theory, the following questions are addressed:

- What is the theory's answer to the central question?
- What is the basic motivation behind that answer?
- What is a precise argument for that answer?
- What are the biggest objections to that answer?
- What are a few good resources for understanding more about the theory?

An additional chapter provides an extensive introduction to the notorious liar paradox. *Truth: The Basics* is an ideal starting point for anyone seeking a lively and accessible introduction to the rich and complex philosophical study of truth.

Jc Beall holds the O'Neill Family Chair in Philosophy at the University of Notre Dame. Beall's principal work is on truth, paradox, logic, and related issues. His publications include *Logical Pluralism* (2005), *Spandrels of Truth* (2009), and *Formal Theories* *of Truth* (2018). In addition, Beall is the author of *Logic: The Basics* (Routledge, 2017).

Ben Middleton has held postdoctoral positions in philosophy at the University of Notre Dame and North Carolina State University. His published papers include work on nonclassical logic and the semantic paradoxes.

THE BASICS SERIES

The Basics is a highly successful series of accessible guidebooks which provide an overview of the fundamental principles of a subject area in a jargon-free and undaunting format.

Intended for students approaching a subject for the first time, the books both introduce the essentials of a subject and provide an ideal springboard for further study. With over 50 titles spanning subjects from artificial intelligence (AI) to women's studies, *The Basics* are an ideal starting point for students seeking to understand a subject area.

Each text comes with recommendations for further study and gradually introduces the complexities and nuances within a subject.

For a full list of titles in this series, please visit www.routledge.com/The-Basics/book-series/B

TRUTH

THE BASICS

Jc Beall and Ben Middleton

Routledge
Taylor & Francis Group

NEW YORK AND LONDON

Designed cover image: Photo by Thomas T on Unsplash

First published 2024
by Routledge
605 Third Avenue, New York, NY 10158

and by Routledge
4 Park Square, Milton Park, Abingdon, Oxon, OX14 4RN

Routledge is an imprint of the Taylor & Francis Group, an informa business

© 2024 Taylor & Francis

The right of Jc Beall and Ben Middleton to be identified as authors of this work has been asserted in accordance with sections 77 and 78 of the Copyright, Designs and Patents Act 1988.

ISBN: 978-1-032-03988-6 (hbk)
ISBN: 978-1-032-03987-9 (pbk)
ISBN: 978-1-003-19010-3 (ebk)

DOI: 10.4324/9781003190103

Typeset in Bembo
by codeMantra

To all who've helped me see truth. — JcB

To Shirley, for her endless love and support. — BM

CONTENTS

INTRODUCTION

1.1 THE CENTRAL QUESTION

This book is an introductory survey of five prominent answers to the *central philosophical question* (henceforth, *central question*) about truth:

(Central Question) What feature do all and only the truths have in common, which makes them all true?

More briefly: what is truth?

A common reaction to the central question is that it's hopelessly deep and complicated, far too complex to answer. This reaction may stem from the following thought. If we could answer the central question correctly, say by identifying Φ as the feature that makes a truth true, then we would thereby be in a position to discover the truth about every *other* subject matter as well. Want to know whether there is extra-terrestrial life? Just test whether 'There is extra-terrestrial life' has Φ. Want to know whether nuclear war will break out this century? Just test whether 'Nuclear war will break out this century' has Φ. Clearly, philosophers cannot hope to discover the truth about *everything*. As a result, philosophers cannot hope to discover the truth about truth either.

The implicit assumption in the preceding argument is that the feature which makes a truth true must be much easier to recognize than

DOI: 10.4324/9781003190103-1

truth itself. Although this would be nice, it need not be the case, and in general, the answers philosophers have given to the central question do not provide us with an algorithm for determining the truth about every conceivable question. This may be disappointing if you had turned to this book to help answer a question in quantum physics, theology, or ethics. On the upside, it makes answering the central question a tractable task, one which philosophers can realistically hope to make progress on.

The first step to answering the central question is to clarify the 'shape' of the question and corresponding answers.

1.2   SHAPE OF THE CENTRAL QUESTION AND THE SORT OF ANSWERS

The central question is one instance of the following general kind of question: what feature do all and only the Fs have in common, which makes them all F? More briefly: what is F? Other questions of this general kind include:

- What feature do all and only the conscious beings have in common, which makes them all conscious?
- What feature do all and only the morally right actions have in common, which makes them all morally right?
- What feature do all and only the blue objects have in common, which makes them all blue?
- What feature do all and only the diamonds have in common, which makes them all diamonds?
- What feature do all and only the hot objects have in common, which makes them all hot?
- For readers with some knowledge of mathematics: what feature do all and only the continuous functions have in common, which makes them all continuous?

The first question has mostly been investigated by philosophers and neuroscientists. No consensus has emerged as to the correct answer, put a popular view is that consciousness consists in certain kinds of complicated information processing.

The second question has mostly been investigated by philosophers and theologians. Again, no consensus has emerged around a single answer, but popular views include the following: the moral rightness of an action consists in it maximizing overall happiness, the moral rightness of an action consists in it being in line with God's commands, and the moral rightness of an action consists in it being what a wholly virtuous person would do.

The third question has mostly been investigated by physicists and philosophers. In this case, something approaching a consensus has emerged around the view that blueness consists in being disposed to reflect light with wavelength between 450 and 495 nanometers under normal conditions.

The fourth and fifth questions have been investigated almost exclusively by physicists. Here, there is complete consensus: being a diamond consists in being composed of carbon atoms arranged in a certain kind of crystal structure, and being a hot object consists in being composed of particles with high mean kinetic energy.

The sixth question has been investigated almost exclusively by mathematicians. Again, here there is complete consensus: being a continuous function consists in being a function for which the preimage of every open set is open. (Do not worry if you do not know what this means.)

An answer to a question of the form 'what is F?' is called an *analysis* of F. We write an analysis of F as follows:

$$x \text{ is } F =_{df} x \text{ is } \Phi$$

where Φ is the feature taken by the analysis to answer the 'what is F?' question. For example, the standard analysis of hotness can be written as:

x is hot $=_{df}$

x is composed of particles with high mean kinetic energy.

As can be seen from the above list, analyses are commonplace both in philosophy and in science more generally. As can also be seen from the above list, the methods used to give an analysis of F vary substantially depending on the domain in which F is found.

Although experimental observations were helpful in analyzing the properties of being hot, being a diamond, and being blue, and likely will be helpful in analyzing consciousness, experimental observations were of no help in analyzing a mathematical function's 'continuity' and are unlikely to be of any help in analyzing moral rightness. Although it is hard to draw the line between domains in which experimental observations are relevant and domains in which they are not, it is safe to say that truth, in this respect, is closer to mathematical continuity than to being a diamond.

Despite the variation in methods used to give analyses, there remain certain abstract features common to all correct analyses (i.e., correct answers to *What is F?* questions), which every analysis aspires to satisfy. We briefly summarize these features below.

1.2.1   EXTENSIONAL ADEQUACY OF CANDIDATE ANSWERS

The most obvious requirement for an analysis of F to be correct is that the feature identified by the analysis is in fact shared by all and only the Fs. This condition is referred to as *extensional adequacy*. For example, an analysis that took consciousness to consist in a certain kind of complicated information processing would not be correct if there were nonconscious beings (computers, perhaps) that perform exactly the same kind of complicated information processing. In other words, the would-be analysis claims that *to be conscious* is just to *process information in such-n-so way*, and so the analysis would be incorrect in the face of such nonconscious information processors.

1.2.2   INTENSIONAL ADEQUACY OF CANDIDATE ANSWERS

Extensional adequacy alone is not enough for an analysis to be correct. For example, for all we know, it might turn out that we on Earth are the only conscious beings in the universe. If this were the case, then the conscious beings would be all and only the animals from Earth. Nevertheless, it would still be incorrect to analyze consciousness as the property of being an animal from Earth. This is because analyzing consciousness as being an animal from Earth entails that it is impossible for a being to be conscious without also being from Earth. Clearly, however, it is *possible* for extra-terrestrial conscious beings to exist, even if, by chance, they do not.

In general, for Φ to be the correct analysis of F, it must be the case that

(i) Φ is *necessary* for F, which means that it is not possible for something to satisfy F without also satisfying Φ.
(ii) Φ is *sufficient* for F, which means that it is not possible for something to satisfy Φ without also satisfying F.

An analysis that satisfies conditions (i) and (ii) is said to be *intensionally adequate*. Note that intensional adequacy entails extensional adequacy, since if, in actual fact, a feature Φ is not shared by all and only the Fs, then Φ is not necessary and sufficient for F. (But, to repeat, extensional adequacy does not entail intensional adequacy.)

1.2.3 EXPLANATORY POWER OF CANDIDATE ANSWERS

Even intensional adequacy is not enough for an analysis to be correct. For example, an analysis of consciousness which took consciousness to consist in *being conscious* would not be correct, despite being intensionally adequate. This is because analyzing consciousness as *being conscious* lacks *explanatory power*, in the sense that we cannot use the analysis to derive any of the known phenomena involving consciousness (e.g., the association between certain kinds of brain processes and certain kinds of conscious states) from more fundamental principles.

Contrast the analysis of consciousness as *being conscious* with the analysis of hotness as *being composed of particles with high mean kinetic energy*. The latter analysis *does* have explanatory power because we can use it to derive various known phenomena involving hotness from more fundamental physical principles. For example, we can derive the conditions under which certain kinds of hot objects will cool down.

In general, for an analysis to be correct, it must have explanatory power.

1.2.4 UNIVOCAL AND NON-UNIVOCAL ANALYSES

We have established that for an analysis to be correct, it must be intensionally (hence extensionally) adequate and have explanatory power. There remains one further point to clarify. All of the proposed analyses listed at the start of this section are *univocal*, which means that they take a single feature to explain the presence of F in all Fs. It could turn out, however, that different kinds of Fs are F for different reasons.

An equivalent way of putting the same point is that the correct analysis of F could have a so-called disjunctive, or *either-or*, form such as

$$x \text{ is } F =_{df} (x \text{ is } \Phi_1) \text{ or } (x \text{ is } \Phi_2) \text{ or } \dots \text{ or } (x \text{ is } \Phi_n)$$

where $\Phi_1, \Phi_2, \dots, \Phi_n$ are different features appropriate for different kinds of Fs. The way we stated the central question seems to presuppose that the correct analysis of truth is univocal; however, univocity is not required of correct analyses. Indeed, all of the analyses of truth considered in this book are non-univocal to some extent, and some are more radically non-univocal than others.

1.3 NECESSARY BACKGROUND ISSUES FOR THE CENTRAL QUESTION

The central question revolves around a fair number of issues from 'truth bearers' to 'context sensitivity'. We address those issues before sketching the plan of the book.

1.3.1 FALSITY

Truth has a natural counterpart: falsity. Consequently, you might expect an analysis of truth to be paired with an analysis of falsity. It turns out, however, that any analysis of truth can straightforwardly be generalized to an analysis of falsity. This is because falsity is plausibly analyzed as follows:

$$x \text{ is false } =_{df} \text{ the negation of } x \text{ is true}$$

where the negation of the sentence 'p' is obtained by prefixing 'p' with the negation operator, namely, 'it is not the case that'.[1] For example, the falsity of the sentence 'It is raining in London' consists in the truth of the sentence 'It is not the case that it is raining in London'. Thus, if Φ is an analysis of truth, then we can substitute 'is Φ' for 'is true' in the above analysis to obtain

$$x \text{ is false } =_{\text{df}} \text{ the negation of } x \text{ is } \Phi.$$

We'll assume such an analysis of falsity throughout.

1.3.2 TRUTH BEARERS

We now turn to issues that arise specifically for the analysis of truth. The first issue: what kinds of objects are true? Equivalently: truth is a property of *what sort of thing*?

In ordinary life, we most commonly predicate truth of two distinct kinds of objects: sentences and beliefs. For example, we can say both that the sentence 'It is raining in London' is true and that Ahmed's belief that it is raining in London is true. It turns out to be more fruitful to focus on the truth of sentences, rather than the truth of beliefs, for two reasons.

The first reason it's more fruitful to focus on sentences than beliefs is that, unlike sentences, which are just finite sequences of symbols, we do not currently have a clear idea of how our beliefs are structured. The most popular contemporary view about beliefs is that our beliefs are something like brain processes. However, we are yet to locate exactly which process in Ahmed's brain is his particular belief that it is raining in London.

The second reason it's more fruitful to focus on sentences than beliefs derives, in a sense, from the first. Because our beliefs are hidden from public view, we developed language in order to share our beliefs. Consequently, every belief is capable of being expressed by a sentence, which is true under exactly the same conditions as the belief it expresses. For example, Ahmed's belief that it is raining in London is expressible by the sentence 'It is raining in London', which, like Ahmed's belief, is true if and only if it is in fact raining in London. Thus, by analyzing truth for sentences, we automatically get an analysis of truth for beliefs: what makes a belief true is being expressible by a true sentence.

Reflecting the foregoing, we assume that the correct analysis of truth has the following non-univocal form:

x is true $=_{df}$ (x is a belief and x is expressible by a true sentence) or

(x is a sentence and x is Φ)

where different theories of truth fill out Φ in different ways.

Having clarified how the analysis of truth for beliefs should go, we will talk about truth in the remainder of the book as if it applied only to sentences.

1.3.3   FOREIGN LANGUAGES

Since people differ in which language they use to express their beliefs, a complete account of truth should explain what the truth of the sentences of each language consists in. However, since languages differ greatly in their syntax, any account of truth which is simultaneously applied to all languages would, by necessity, have a very abstract character. Consequently, we prefer to analyze truth for each language separately.

Given that this book is written in English, we focus on how to analyze truth for sentences of English. It is important to clarify, however, that we do not take the truth of sentences of English to be more fundamental than the truth of sentences of, say, German, Hindi, or Mandarin Chinese. In particular, we do not suppose that the correct account of truth for, say, German is the property of being synonymous with a true sentence of English. Rather, we suppose that the correct analysis of truth for sentences has the form:

x is true $=_{df}$ (x is a sentence of English and x is Φ_1) or

(x is a sentence of German and x is Φ_2) or

(x is a sentence of Hindi and x is Φ_3) or

(x is a sentence of Mandarin Chinese and x is Φ_4) or...

where $\Phi_1, \Phi_2, \Phi_3, \Phi_4, \ldots$ are distinct yet structurally similar properties. Since this book is written at an introductory level, we do not attempt to generalize the theories of truth for English surveyed here to other languages. Nevertheless, we hope the reader will not be left in doubt that this could in principle be done.

For ease of expression, we will talk about truth in the remainder of the book as if it applied only to sentences of English.

1.3.4 SCOPE AMBIGUITY

Is the following sentence true?

The Earth is flat and the Earth is circular or the Earth is spherical.

The correct answer is: *it depends*. In particular, the truth status of the sentence depends on how the different components of the sentence are grouped together. We can use brackets to make clear the possible groupings:

1. (The Earth is flat and the Earth is circular) or the Earth is spherical.
2. The Earth is flat and (the Earth is circular or the Earth is spherical).

When grouped according to (1), the sentence asserts that one of the following conditions obtains: (i) the Earth is flat and circular, (ii) the Earth is spherical. Since condition (ii) *does* obtain, the sentence is true according to grouping (1).

By contrast, when grouped according to (2), the sentence asserts that both of the following conditions obtain: (i) the Earth is flat, and (ii) the Earth is circular or spherical. Since condition (i) does *not* obtain, the sentence is not true according to grouping (2).

Because sentences of English frequently admit different possible groupings, and the way a sentence is grouped can affect its truth status, a theory of truth should, strictly speaking, apply to sentences that have been bracketed to force a unique grouping. However, since this book is written at an introductory level, we will mostly gloss over this issue, leaving the brackets implicit.

1.3.5   LEXICAL AMBIGUITY

Scope ambiguity is not the only kind of ambiguity found in language – there is also *lexical* ambiguity. To understand lexical ambiguity, consider whether the following sentence is true:

A bank is usually a good place to fish.

As before, the correct answer is: *it depends*. However, on this occasion, whether the sentence is true does not depend on how it is grouped, but rather on how the word 'bank' is interpreted.

In English, the word 'bank' has at least two possible interpretations: (i) a type of financial institution and (ii) a type of geographical area – in particular, the type of geographical area which immediately borders a river. According to interpretation (i), the sentence is false – financial institutions, after all, do not usually contain fish. By contrast, according to interpretation (ii), the sentence is true, since rivers do usually contain fish.

Just as we can resolve scope ambiguities by adding appropriate brackets, we can resolve lexical ambiguities by adding appropriate indices to ambiguous words and then providing a key that informs us which interpretation the indices refer to. For example, in the case of 'bank', our key would contain the following two entries:

bank$_1$:   The type of financial institution in which money is deposited.

bank$_2$:   The type of geographical area that borders a river.

We can then enforce a disambiguation of 'bank' by adding the appropriate index:

A bank$_2$ is usually a good place to fish.

Given that many words in English admit multiple possible interpretations, and how we choose to interpret those words can affect the truth status of a sentence in which they appear, a theory of truth should, strictly speaking, apply to *fully disambiguated sentences* – sentences that have *both* been bracketed to resolve all scope ambiguities and, in addition, had indices added to resolve all lexical ambiguities. However, since this book is written at an introductory level, we will, like the brackets, leave the indices implicit.

1.3.6 TWO KINDS OF EQUIVALENCE

Before introducing the next key feature of truth, we need to clarify some terminology.

We say the condition that *p* is *materially equivalent* to the condition that *q* when in actual fact, either both conditions obtain or both conditions fail to obtain. For example, supposing we are alone in the universe, the condition that there is a conscious being in the room is materially equivalent to the condition that there is an animal from Earth in the room. The sentence '*p* if and only if *q*' asserts that the condition that *p* is materially equivalent to the condition that *q*.

We say the condition that *p* is *necessarily equivalent* to the condition that *q* when in every possible world, either both conditions obtain or both conditions fail to obtain. Necessary equivalence is much more demanding than material equivalence. For example, because there is a possible world in which intelligent extra-terrestrial life exists, the condition that there is a conscious being in the room is not necessarily equivalent to the condition that there is an animal from Earth in the room. The sentence 'Necessarily, *p* if and only if *q*' asserts that the condition that *p* is necessarily equivalent to the condition that *q*.

1.3.7 TRUTH CONDITIONS

The most central feature of truth is that the truth of each sentence '*p*' is materially equivalent to the condition that *p*. For example, the truth of 'It is raining in London' is materially equivalent to the condition that it is raining in London, the truth of 'Unemployment is falling in the US' is materially equivalent to the condition that unemployment is falling in the US, and the truth of 'The average temperature on Earth is rising' is materially equivalent to the condition that the average temperature on Earth is rising.

Consequently, truth satisfies the following principle, which is referred to in philosophy as the *T-schema*:

'*p*' is true if and only if *p*.

The T-schema might initially strike you as a mere tautology, about as informative as the principle that *p* if and only if *p*. But appearances can be misleading, and in this case they are. If the T-schema strikes you as tautologous, then this is only because you speak English. Consider, for example, the following instance of the T-schema:

'It is raining in London' is true if and only if it is raining in London.

If you translate this sentence into, say, French, then it would strike a French speaker as far from trivial. This can be seen by going the other way around and translating the corresponding French instance of the T-schema into English:

'Il pleut à Londres' is true if and only if it is raining in London.

It should now be clear that, far from being a tautology, the T-schema asserts a non-trivial equivalence between a linguistic condition on the one hand and a 'worldly' condition on the other hand. We refer to the condition that *p* as the *truth condition* of the sentence '*p*', since it is the worldly condition under which '*p*', in actual fact, is true.

1.3.8   THE LIAR PARADOX

Because the T-schema captures the most central feature of truth, it is a basic requirement on the correctness of an analysis of truth as Φ that Φ satisfies the analogous Φ-schema:

'*p*' is Φ if and only if *p*.

Thus, the instances of the Φ-schema should at least be consistent with our background knowledge. It turns out, however, that the T-schema runs into consistency problems all by itself, and the consistency problems for the T-schema automatically transfer to the Φ-schema for any other choice of Φ. Consequently, these problems need to be resolved, or at least appropriately contained, before we can attempt to analyze truth.

The T-schema runs into consistency problems when we attempt to predicate truth of sentences that themselves contain the predicate 'is true'. Suppose, for example, that we give the name 'The Liar' to the sentence 'The Liar is not true'. By instantiating the T-schema, we get

'The Liar is not true' is true if and only if The Liar is not true.

Consequently, since The Liar *just is* the sentence 'The Liar is not true', we get

The Liar is true if and only if The Liar is not true

which, according to the orthodox account of logic, is impossible.

Since we should reject any theory that entails an impossibility, we must either reject the orthodox account of logic or else restrict the T-schema to some privileged subset of sentences. We postpone a full discussion of the issues involved in rejecting the orthodox account of logic to accommodate the unrestricted T-schema to Chapter 7. Until then, we restrict our attention to only the correct account of truth for sentences that do not themselves contain the predicate 'is true', for which the liar paradox does not arise.

⋆ ⋆ *Parenthetical note: A further slightly technical restriction.* Since replacing 'is true' in the unrestricted T-schema with any other predicate also runs afoul of the liar paradox, we need to further restrict our attention to sentences that do not contain our proposed analysis of truth. Therefore, we assume that the correct analysis of truth for English has the form:

x is true $=_{df}$ (x contains no truth-related notions and x is Φ_1) or

(x contains truth-related notions and x is Φ_2)

and, until Chapter 7, restrict our attention to filling out Φ_1. For ease of expression, until Chapter 7, we will talk as if truth only applied to sentences that do not themselves contain any truth-related notions. *End note.* ⋆ ⋆

1.3.8.1 Tarski on Extensional Adequacy

Suppose Φ is an analysis of truth. As previously argued, at a minimum all instances of the Φ-schema:

$$\text{`}p\text{' is } \Phi \text{ if and only if } p,$$

where 'p' contains no truth-related notions, should be consistent with our background knowledge. But it would be better if not only were the instances of the Φ-schema consistent with our background knowledge, but our background knowledge actively *entailed* the instances of the Φ-schema. This is for two reasons.

First, if our background knowledge entails the instances of the Φ-schema, then analyzing truth as Φ has explanatory power, because it explains *why* the T-schema holds. This is analogous to the way in which the analysis of being a diamond as being composed of carbon atoms arranged in a certain kind of crystal structure has explanatory power in virtue of entailing various observable properties of diamonds (their color, hardness, ability to conduct heat, and so on).

The second reason why it is better for our background knowledge to entail the instances of the Φ-schema is more subtle. The first person to grasp this reason was the Polish logician Alfred Tarski, who has done more than anyone to advance our understanding of truth. What Tarski understood was that if our background knowledge entails all instances of the Φ-schema, then we thereby have a theoretical guarantee that the analysis of truth as Φ is extensionally adequate, which, recall, means that all and only the truths have Φ. This is because, for any sentence 'p', it follows from:

$$\text{`}p\text{' is } \Phi \text{ if and only if } p$$

and

$$\text{`}p\text{' is true if and only if } p$$

that

$$\text{`}p\text{' is true if and only if `}p\text{' is } \Phi.$$

The fact that we have a theoretical method of guaranteeing the extensional adequacy of an analysis of truth is a remarkable fact, which distinguishes the analysis of truth from most other cases of analysis. In particular, there is no theoretical method of guaranteeing the extensional adequacy of an analysis of consciousness, or of moral rightness, or even of blueness. In these cases, we argue for the extensional adequacy of an analysis of F as Φ by, in effect, checking that each object in a large sample of Fs has Φ, and each object in a large sample of non-Fs lacks Φ. Clearly, Tarski's method is a vast improvement over such a piecemeal approach.

1.3.9   CONTEXT SENSITIVITY

Consider the following puzzle. John is a $6'2''$ professional basketball player. Mary points to John while he is playing basketball and asserts 'That guy is not tall'. In contrast, Kylie points to John while he is shopping at the mall and asserts 'That guy is tall'. On the surface, these two assertions are incompatible – John cannot be both tall and not tall. Yet, we are also inclined to accept that both Mary and Kylie speak truly. So what gives?

The solution to this puzzle is probably already apparent to you. The predicate 'is tall' is *context sensitive*, in the sense that its meaning depends on the context in which it is used. When Mary says 'John is not tall', she means that John is not tall *for a male basketball player*. Since John's height is below the average height of a male basketball player, what Mary says is correct.

By contrast, when Kylie says 'John is tall', she means that John is tall *for a male shopper at the mall*. Since John's height is significantly above the average height of a male shopper at the mall, what Kylie says is also correct. Thus, despite the superficial appearance of conflict, there is in fact no disagreement between Mary's statement and Kylie's statement.

★ ★ *Parenthetical note: The difference between lexical ambiguity and context sensitivity.* You might be wondering how context sensitivity differs from lexical ambiguity. What is the difference between the context sensitivity of 'tall' and the lexical ambiguity of 'bank'?

The answer is that, unlike 'bank', whether 'tall' applies to a particular object on a given occasion of use depends *in a systematic way* on the context in which 'tall' is used. In particular, the context of use provides a *reference class* of objects – the objects the conversational participants are talking about – and 'tall' applies to an object in that context if and only if the height of the object in question is sufficiently above the average height of the reference class.

By contrast, no systematic story can be given as to whether 'bank' applies to financial banks or river banks on a particular occasion of use – it is largely just a matter of what the speaker has in mind. *End note.* ★ ★

Since the instances of the T-schema should hold in every context, it follows that 'is true' inherits all of the context sensitivity present in the language to which it is applied. For example, because Mary would be correct to assert 'John is not tall', she would also be correct to assert "The sentence 'John is tall' is not true". Likewise, because Kylie would be correct to assert 'John is tall', she would also be correct to assert "The sentence 'John is tall' is true". Consequently, to assert "The sentence 'p' is true" in context C is to assert that 'p' is true relative to C.

In particular, when Mary says "The sentence 'John is tall' is not true", she thereby asserts that 'John is tall' is not true in her present context, in which the standard for tallness is determined by the set of all male basketball players. Similarly, when Kylie says "The sentence 'John is tall' is true", she thereby asserts that 'John is tall' is true in *her* present context, in which the standard for tallness is determined by the set of all male shoppers at the mall. Again, the appearance of conflict between Mary's statement and Kylie's statement dissipates.

Given that "The sentence 'p' is true" means in context C that 'p' is true relative to C, you might expect that an analysis of truth would have the form

$$x \text{ is true relative to context } C =_{df} x \text{ stands in relation } R \text{ to } C.$$

Although some philosophers favor analyzing truth in this manner, this is not the approach we take in this book. Instead, we only survey analyses of truth with the form:

$$x \text{ is true} =_{df} x \text{ is } \Phi$$

where the context used to interpret sentences has been implicitly fixed in the background. There are two main reasons for favoring our approach.

First, since we do not need to account for the parameter C, the resulting theories of truth are considerably simpler. This suits the introductory nature of this book.

Second, one of the leading theories of truth – the *transparency* theory – can only be formulated when the context for interpreting sentences is implicitly fixed in the background. Although some philosophers take this to count against the transparency theory, it is better to adopt a framework that does not, from the outset, rule out the possibility that the transparency theory is the correct theory of truth.

1.3.10 RELATIVISM

Roughly speaking, relativism about truth is the thesis that sentences are not true absolutely, but rather are only true relative to some other factor. One way to make this thesis precise is to take the other factor to be the context in which the sentence is used. Under this interpretation, relativism about truth is the thesis that whether a sentence is true depends on the context in which it is used.

As we saw in the previous section, this version of relativism about truth is unquestionably correct. To take an uncontroversial example, suppose Dan and Zoe are wearing blue and red shirts, respectively. At the very same moment of time, Dan and Zoe both utter the sentence 'I am wearing a blue shirt'. In this case, despite uttering the very same sentence, Dan says something true but Zoe says something *un*true.

This discrepancy arises because the context in which a sentence is used – more specifically, the identity of the speaker of the sentence – determines who the indexical expression 'I' refers to. Relative to a context in which the speaker is Dan, 'I' refers to Dan and so, since Dan is in fact wearing a blue shirt, the sentence 'I am wearing a blue shirt' is true. Likewise, relative to a context in which the speaker is Zoe, 'I' refers to Zoe and so, since Zoe is not in fact wearing a blue shirt, the sentence 'I am wearing a blue shirt' fails to be true.

Relativism about truth is generally taken to be a radical, counterintuitive doctrine. Thus, identifying relativism about truth with the uncontroversial thesis that truth depends on context does not do justice to what proponents of relativism about truth intend their view to be. A full discussion of how best to understand relativism about truth is beyond the scope of this book. However, we will briefly discuss two alternative ways of making relativism about truth precise, which strike us as better approximations of what relativists intend.

According to the first, more radical way of understanding relativism about truth, relativism about truth is the thesis that, even if we were to remove all context sensitivity from the part of English which does not contain any truth-related notions, 'is true' would remain context sensitive. That is to say, even if we were to remove indexical expressions, such as 'I', 'you', and 'that', and non-truth-related context sensitive predicates, such as 'tall', 'thin', and 'old', whether 'is true' applies to a sentence would still depend on the context in which 'is true' is used. Therefore, on this understanding, relativists about truth consider 'is true' to be an *independent* source of context sensitivity, over and above the context sensitivity present in the non-truth-related part of language.

For example, a relativist of this kind might maintain that, even though the sentence 'Mount Everest is taller than K2' is not context sensitive, the sentence

'Mount Everest is taller than K2' is true

is context sensitive, since its meaning relies on some contextual information. This contextual information is traditionally taken to be something like the way the user of the sentence conceptualizes the world. On this view, even when we remove all the context sensitivity in 'p', there is still no sense in which 'p' could be true absolutely – the most we can say is that 'p' is true relative to one of the many possible conceptualizations of reality.

Call this version of relativism *strong* relativism about truth. Although strong relativism might seem plausible, it can easily be refuted. To see how, imagine that Miho and Shirley are two speakers of English who conceptualize the world in different ways. At the very same moment of time, Miho asserts *The sentence 'Mount Everest is taller than K2' is true*, while Shirley asserts *The sentence 'Mount Everest is taller than K2' is not true*, where we assume that 'Mount Everest is taller than K2' is not context sensitive.

According to the strong relativist, Miho and Shirley could both be right. Yet, this cannot be. For if Miho is right then, by the T-schema, she would also be right in asserting *Mount Everest is taller than K2*. Likewise, if Shirley is right, then, by the T-schema, she would also be right in asserting *Mount Everest is not taller than K2*. But then, given our assumption that 'Mount Everest is taller than K2' is not context sensitive, we can infer that at the time Miho and Shirley make their assertions, Mount Everest both is and is not taller than K2, which is impossible.[2]

So the relativist about truth cannot allow the context sensitivity of 'is true' to float free of the context sensitivity of the underlying language. Nevertheless, it remains an open possibility that the non-truth-related predicates in our language are more context sensitive than we ordinarily assume – so that, for example, 'Mount Everest is taller than K2' means in a given context that Mount Everest is taller than K2 *relative to* the speaker's way of conceptualizing reality. This entails the truth of 'Mount Everest is taller than K2' is also relative to a conceptualization – but only because *being taller than* is already relative to a conceptualization. On this view, truth is radically relative, not in virtue of anything intrinsic to *truth*, but rather in virtue of the language to which it is applied.

By adding the speaker's way of conceptualizing the world to the context for determining the meaning of a sentence, relativists can do justice to the radical nature of relativism about truth, while maintaining our ordinary understanding of the nature of truth. Consequently, everything we say in this book is compatible with this version of relativism about truth (recall from the previous section we assume the context for determining the meaning of a sentence is implicitly fixed in the background).

1.4 PLAN OF THE BOOK

Having addressed the various background issues around the central question of truth, we now turn to answers. In this book, we discuss five major answers to the central question:

1. **Correspondence**. According to the correspondence answer, truth consists in correspondence to the facts, where facts are understood to be the existing portions of reality.

2. **Semantic**. According to the semantic answer, the meanings of the simple words in a sentence combine to directly associate a sentence with its truth condition. A sentence is then 'made true' by its truth condition 'obtaining'.

3. **Verifiability**. According to the verifiability answer, every sentence is associated with a procedure and an outcome, such that if following the procedure were to result in the outcome, the community of speakers would agree to accept the sentence. The truth of a sentence then consists in the condition that following its associated procedure would result in its associated outcome, regardless of whether the procedure is ever actually followed.

4. **Transparency**. According to the transparency answer, to assert that 'p' is true *just is* to assert that p. Consequently, there is no single feature common to all truths which explains why they are true. Instead, any explanation of *why 'p' is true* is an explanation of *why p* (so to speak). For example, an explanation of why 'Sea water is salty' is true is an explanation of why sea water is salty, an explanation of why 'The Earth revolves around the Sun' is true is an explanation of why the Earth revolves around the Sun, and so on.

5. **Plurality**. According to the plurality answer, different accounts of truth are required for sentences with different subject matters. For example, while the correspondence answer is suitable for sentences about (say) ordinary macroscopic reality, the verifiability answer is more suitable for sentences about (say) mathematical, ethical, or microscopic reality.

Multiple different versions of each of these five answers can be found in the philosophical literature, and philosophers who propose the same general answer to the central question may nevertheless have substantial theoretical disagreements. Since this is an introductory book, we do not in any fashion attempt to cover all of the internal disagreements between proponents of the same general answer. Instead, we offer very simplified, yet sufficiently precise, formulations of what we take to be representative versions of each of the five answers outlined above. There may well be (in fact, probably is) no actual theorist who holds exactly the sketched representative view;

however, the representative views give a sufficient family resemblance to important actual answers that are advanced by actual theorists.

To aid the reader in comparing the five answers, every chapter has the same structure:

1. **Answer to the central question**. In this section, we outline the analysis of truth on offer.
2. **Motivation**. In this section, we explain why philosophers have been interested in the analysis.
3. **Argument**. In this section, we present an argument for the target analysis.
4. **Evaluation**. In this section, we do two things. First, we consider some objections to the argument offered in the previous section. Second, we consider some objections to the analysis itself, which apply regardless of the argument used in support of it.

In Chapter 7, after evaluating each of the five candidate answers to the central question, we take up the challenge of answering the liar paradox. This chapter is more technical in nature than the chapters that precede it, and many of the issues raised in the final chapter are to a large extent independent of the issues raised in the rest of the book. Nevertheless, since any adequate theory of truth must ultimately apply to the entirety of English, tackling the liar paradox is a task that every truth theorist – regardless of whether they endorse the correspondence, semantic, verifiability, transparency, or plurality answer – must eventually undertake.

At the end of the book, you can find various technical appendices that are referenced throughout the text. These offer a more advanced discussion of some topics discussed in the book and are generally suitable for readers with prior knowledge of philosophy and formal logic.

1.5 CHAPTER SUMMARY

In this chapter, we introduced the central question of the book: what is the feature shared by all and only the truths, which makes them all true? We explained that for an answer to the central question to be correct, it must be intensionally adequate and have explanatory power. We also clarified some necessary background issues regarding truth. In particular, we clarified that, in this book, we take truth to primarily be a property of sentences, rather than beliefs. In addition, we pointed out that the most central feature of truth – consequently, the feature of truth most in need of explanation – is the T-schema:

'p' is true if and only if p.

NOTES

1. It should be noted that analyzing falsity in this manner is philosophically controversial.
2. See Appendix A (page 155) for a more precise formulation of this argument.

FURTHER READING

- For further discussion of the nature of analysis, see Gideon Rosen, 'Real Definition', *Analytic Philosophy*, Vol. 56, No. 3, pp. 189–209, 2015.
- For further discussion of the T-schema, see Sections 1 (pp. 154 – 165) and 3 (pp.186 –209) of Alfred Tarski, 'The Concept of Truth in Formalized Languages', in *Logic, Semantics, Metamathematics* (Hackett Publishing Company: Oxford, 1956).
- For further discussion of relativism, see Herman Cappelen and Torfinn Thomesen Huvenes, 'Relative Truth', in Michael Glanzberg (ed.), *The Oxford Handbook of Truth* (Oxford University Press: Oxford, 2018), pp. 517–542.

CORRESPONDENCE

2.1 ANSWER TO THE CENTRAL QUESTION

According to the correspondence theory, for a sentence to be true is for it to correspond to some existing portion of reality. For example, the sentence 'There are wild elephants in Africa' is true because it corresponds to the portion of reality consisting of wild elephants in Africa. In contrast, the sentence 'There are wild elephants in Belgium' is untrue because it fails to correspond to any existing portion of reality.

The technical term for a portion of reality is a *fact*. When formulated in terms of facts, the correspondence theory offers the following answer to our central question:

(Correspondence Theory) x is true $=_{df} x$ corresponds to a fact.

The correspondence theory may initially strike you as obviously correct. After all, we ordinarily think of the true sentences as those sentences that accurately map the contours of reality, and the correspondence theory appears to give expression to this ordinary view. However, while it is undoubtedly correct that the true sentences *in some sense* match up with reality, it is on reflection not clear that the

DOI: 10.4324/9781003190103-2

correspondence theory is the best way of making this idea precise. This is because the correspondence theory commits us to an unusual class of theoretical entities – *facts* – whose existence is far from obvious. In the remainder of this section, we describe in more detail the category of facts and the relation of correspondence.

2.1.1 FACTS

According to the correspondence theory, reality naturally divides into chunks, called *facts*, which sentences are able to correspond to. When a sentence '*p*' corresponds to a fact Φ, we say that Φ is a *truthmaker* for '*p*', since Φ is an entity out in the world whose existence is responsible for making '*p*' true.

Although facts contain the ordinary objects of common sense and scientific inquiry – objects such as trees, cars, mountains, clouds, tigers, rocks, molecules, and atoms – a fact cannot be identified with the ordinary objects it contains. This is because a fact, by its very nature, cannot survive all possible changes the objects it contains can undergo.

Consider, for example, the sentence 'It is cloudy in Austin'. Suppose this sentence is true. Then, according to the correspondence theory, it corresponds to some fact – mostly plausibly, a fact describable as *clouds covering Austin*. Now suppose that, over the course of the day, the clouds above Austin gradually drift away, leaving behind clear blue sky. Then, the sentence 'It is cloudy in Austin' would cease to be true, and so, its truthmaker would cease to exist. Nevertheless, the clouds and Austin still exist – they are just in different places. Consequently, a fact describable as *clouds covering Austin* is something over and above Austin and the clouds that temporarily cover it.

This observation generalizes. Unlike the dog and his bed, a fact describable as *the dog being in his bed* cannot survive the dog getting out of his bed. Unlike Anika's left arm, a fact describable as *Anika's left arm being raised* cannot survive Anika lowering her left arm. Unlike London and the relevant H_2O molecules, a fact describable as *the falling of rain in London* cannot survive the stopping of rain in London.

So, a fact is something over and above the objects it contains. But then what kind of entity is a fact? Correspondence theorists generally answer this question as follows: facts are structured entities composed of one or more objects and their collective state, just as a broom is composed of a handle and a brush. For example, a fact describable as *Anika's left arm being raised* is a structured entity composed of Anika's left arm and the abstract property of being raised; a fact describable as *Miami being humid* is a structured entity composed of Miami and the abstract property of humidity; a fact describable as *the dog being in his bed* is a structured entity composed of the dog, the dog's bed and the abstract relation of containment.

For correspondence theorists, reality is the totality of existing facts − a vast mosaic of ordinary objects enveloped in state − and reality changes as old facts go out of existence and are replaced by new facts. When ordinary objects change, they cease to be part of the old facts and become part of the new facts instead. For example, when Frankie, the dog, is asleep, he is part of a fact composed of Frankie and the property of sleeping, which goes out of existence when Frankie wakes up, at which point Frankie becomes part of a new fact, composed of Frankie and the property of wakefulness.

Most correspondence theorists posit two basic kinds of fact: *relational* facts and *non-relational* facts. A non-relational fact is a fact composed of a single object and a single property. Examples of non-relational facts include the fact of Anika's left arm being raised, the fact of Miami being humid and the fact of the lake being frozen.

In contrast, a relational fact is a fact composed of multiple objects, arranged in a particular order, and a single relation. For example, the fact of Canada being north of Mexico is a relational fact composed of Canada and Mexico, arranged in that order, plus the relation of *being north of*. Changing the order of the objects in a relational fact usually results a different fact. For example, if we reversed the order of Canada and Mexico in the fact of Canada being north of Mexico, we would obtain the fact of Mexico being north of Canada, which does not exist.

2.1.2 CORRESPONDENCE

Whether a sentence '*p*' corresponds to a particular fact depends on two factors:

1. the meanings of the basic constituents of 'p'
2. the syntactic structure of 'p' – i.e., the way in which those basic constituents are arranged.

To take a simple example, 'France is more populous than Spain' corresponds to the fact of France being more populous than Spain because its basic constituents ('France', 'is more populous than', 'Spain') refer to the basic constituents of the corresponding fact (France, *being more populous than*, Spain) and the way in which the constituents of the sentence are arranged mirrors the structure of the fact itself. In this section, we explain in more detail how factors (1) and (2) determine correspondence.

2.1.2.1 The Meanings of the Basic Constituents

Sentences contain two kinds of basic constituents: names (such as 'Obama', 'France', and 'Mars') and predicates (such as 'is heavy', 'is cold', and 'is close to'). Predicates in turn divide into two kinds: *monadic* predicates and *polyadic* predicates, which we define below. In this subsection, we explain what the meanings of these basic constituents are.

2.1.2.1.1 Names   The meaning of a name is simply the object it refers to. For example, the meaning of 'Obama' is Obama, the meaning of 'France' is France, and the meaning of 'Mars' is Mars.

2.1.2.1.2 Monadic Predicates   A monadic predicate is a linguistic object that combines with a single name to produce a sentence. For example, 'is a capital city' is a monadic predicate, because it combines with the name 'Tokyo' to produce the sentence 'Tokyo is a capital city'; 'is frozen over' is a monadic predicate, because it combines with the name 'The Arctic Ocean' to produce the sentence 'The Arctic Ocean is frozen over'; and 'is a gas giant' is a monadic predicate, because it combines with the name 'Jupiter' to produce the sentence 'Jupiter is a gas giant'.

The majority view among philosophers is that the meaning of a monadic predicate is an abstract property, which can simultaneously be instantiated by multiple different objects. For example, the meaning of 'is a capital city' is the property of being a capital city, which is simultaneously instantiated by Tokyo, London, and Buenos Aires. The meaning of 'is frozen over' is the property of being frozen over, which during northern winter is simultaneously instantiated by the Arctic Ocean, a large number of different lakes, and a large number of different rivers. The meaning of the monadic predicate 'is a gas giant' is the property of being a gas giant, which is simultaneously instantiated by Jupiter and Saturn. Just as names refer to objects, monadic predicates refer to properties.

2.1.2.1.3 Polyadic Predicates A polyadic predicate is a linguistic object that combines with multiple names to produce a sentence. In particular, an n-place predicate is a linguistic object that combines with exactly n names to produce a sentence. For example, 'is north of' is a 2-place predicate, because it combines with the names 'Canada' and 'Mexico' to produce the sentence 'Canada is north of Mexico'; 'was president of...in the year' is a 3-place predicate, because it combines with the names 'JFK', 'the US', and '1961' to produce the sentence 'JFK was president of the US in the year 1961'; and 'is warmer than' is a 2-place predicate, because it combines with the names 'Chicago' and 'London' to produce the sentence 'Chicago is warmer than London'.

The majority view among philosophers is that the meaning of an n-place predicate is an abstract n-place relation, which can simultaneously relate multiple different groups of n objects. For example, the meaning of 'is north of' is the 2-place relation of being north of, which simultaneously relates Canada to Mexico, Indonesia to Australia, and Scotland to England. The meaning of 'was president of...in the year' is the 3-place relation of being president of the country c in the year y, which simultaneously relates JFK to the United States and 1961, Charles de Gaulle to France and 1968, and Obama to the United States and 2009. The meaning of 'is warmer than' is the 2-place relation of being warmer than, which simultaneously relates (at the time of writing) Las Vegas to Chicago, Chicago to London, and London to Reykjavik. Just as names refer to objects and monadic predicates refer to properties, n-place predicates refer to n-place relations.

2.1.2.2 The Contribution of Syntactic Structure

As discussed in the introduction, the essential feature of truth – the feature every analysis of truth ought to explain – is that for each sentence 'p',

(T-schema)   'p' is true if and only if p.

The correspondence theory asserts that 'p' is true if and only if 'p' corresponds to a fact. Consequently, for the correspondence theory to explain the T-schema, it must be independently plausible that 'p' corresponds to a fact if and only if p. Call this principle the *correspondence schema*.

Whether a sentence satisfies the correspondence schema depends on the nature of the correspondence relation. In particular, whether a sentence satisfies the correspondence schema depends on how the meanings of the basic constituents of the sentence combine to determine which fact, if any, the sentence corresponds to. In this section, we show that, given reasonable background assumptions about facts, there exists a natural theory of correspondence according to which a non-trivial subset of sentences satisfy the correspondence schema.[3]

2.1.2.2.1 Atomic Sentences   An *atomic* sentence is a sentence either of the form 't is F', where t is a name and F is a monadic predicate, or of the form '$t_1,...,t_n$ are R-related', where $t_1,...,t_n$ are names and R is an n-place predicate. For example, 'Obama was president', 'Glasgow is in Scotland', and 'The Earth is closer than Jupiter to the Sun' are all atomic sentences.

For the sake of brevity, we follow the convention of treating 't is F' as the special case of '$t_1,...,t_n$ are R-related' where $n = 1$ (and so, somewhat awkwardly, treat properties as 1-place relations). With this convention in place, we can give a uniform analysis of correspondence for atomic sentences:

(Atomic Correspondence)   '$t_1,...,t_n$ are R-related' corresponds to Φ $=_{\mathrm{df}}$ Φ is composed of the objects which $t_1,...,t_n$ refer to (arranged in that order) and the relation which R refers to.

According to this analysis, what it takes for 'Miami is humid' to correspond to Φ is for Φ to be composed of the object which 'Miami' refers to (viz., Miami) and the property which 'is humid' refers to (viz., humidity). Similarly, what it takes for 'France is more populous than Spain' to correspond to Φ is for Φ to be composed of the objects which 'France' and 'Spain' refer to (viz., France and Spain), arranged in that order, plus the relation which 'is more populous than' refers to (viz., *being more populous than*).

The analysis of correspondence for atomic sentences entails that there is a deep similarity between the internal structure of an atomic sentence and the internal structure of the fact to which it corresponds. For example, 'Miami is humid' is composed of the linguistic constituents 'Miami' and 'is humid', while the fact of Miami being humid is composed of the worldly constituents Miami and humidity. Similarly, 'France is more populous than Spain' is composed of 'France', 'is more populous than', and 'Spain', with 'France' preceding 'Spain' in the sentence, while the fact of France being more populous than Spain is composed of France and Spain, arranged in that order, plus the relation of *being more populous than*. Supposing, as the correspondence theory does, that truth *just is* correspondence, the structural similarity between an atomic truth and its truthmaker aligns closely with the common sense view that the true sentences are those that match reality.

The analysis of correspondence for atomic sentences entails that atomic sentences satisfy the correspondence schema. To take an arbitrary example, consider the sentence 'The Pacific Ocean is frozen over'. By the analysis of correspondence, 'The Pacific Ocean is frozen over' corresponds to a fact if and only if there exists a fact composed of the object which 'The Pacific Ocean' refers to and the property which 'is frozen over' refers to. Since 'The Pacific Ocean' refers to the Pacific Ocean and 'is frozen over' refers to the property of being frozen over, we can infer that 'The Pacific Ocean is frozen over' corresponds to a fact if and only if there exists a fact composed of the Pacific Ocean and the property of being frozen over. Consequently, by the nature of facts, 'The Pacific Ocean is frozen over' corresponds to a fact if and only if the Pacific Ocean is frozen over.

Since the analysis of correspondence entails that atomic sentences satisfy the correspondence schema, the correspondence theory (in combination with the background theory of facts and correspondence) *explains* the T-schema for atomic sentences. For example, the explanation for why 'The Pacific Ocean is frozen over' is true if and only if the Pacific Ocean is frozen over is that (i) truth *just is* correspondence and (ii) 'The Pacific Ocean is frozen over' corresponds to a fact if and only if the Pacific Ocean is frozen over.

2.1.2.2.2 Disjunctions of Atomic Sentences To derive the instances of the correspondence schema for sentences of the form 'α or β', where α and β are atomic sentences, we first need to specify the analysis of correspondence for sentences formed by the connective 'or', which are known as *disjunctions*. In this case, the analysis is easy to state:

(Disjunctive Correspondence)   'p or q' corresponds to $\Phi =_{df}$ either 'p' corresponds to Φ or 'q' corresponds to Φ.

For example, 'Chicago is windy or London is windy' corresponds to any fact which 'Chicago is windy' corresponds to, any fact which 'London is windy' corresponds to, and nothing else.

In combination with the analysis of correspondence for atomic sentences, the analysis of correspondence for disjunctions entails the correspondence schema for disjunctions of atomic sentences. To take an arbitrary example, reconsider the sentence 'Chicago is windy or London is windy'. By the analysis of correspondence for disjunctions, 'Chicago is windy or London is windy' corresponds to a fact if and only if either 'Chicago is windy' corresponds to a fact or 'London is windy' corresponds to a fact. By the analysis of correspondence for atomic sentences, 'Chicago is windy' corresponds to a fact if and only if Chicago is windy, and 'London is windy' corresponds to a fact if and only if London is windy. Consequently, 'Chicago is windy or London is windy' corresponds to a fact if and only if either Chicago is windy or London is windy.

2.1.2.2.3 Conjunctions of Atomic Sentences Following the example of 'or', one might expect the analysis of correspondence for sentences formed by the connective 'and', which are known as *conjunctions*, to be:

(#1) 'p and q' corresponds to $\Phi =_{\mathrm{df}}$ both 'p' corresponds to Φ and 'q' corresponds to Φ.

The problem with (#1) is that there will not in general be enough facts to cover all true conjunctions. Consider, for example, the true sentence 'Miami is humid and the Muir Glacier is melting'. Even if we grant there exists a fact **Miami** which 'Miami is humid' corresponds to, and a fact **Muir** which 'The Muir Glacier is melting' corresponds to, neither **Miami** nor **Muir** is such that *both* 'Miami is humid' and 'The Muir Glacier is melting' correspond to it, since **Miami** entirely concerns Miami and **Muir** entirely concerns the Muir Glacier.

The general problem is that a truthmaker for 't is F' is composed entirely of the object which t refers to and the property which F refers to. This entails that correspondence for atomic sentences is *exact*, in the sense that the truthmaker for an atomic sentence cannot contain objects or state the sentence is not directly about. Thus, when 't is F' and 's is G' have different subject matters, they will not correspond to the same fact. They could, however, correspond to different facts. In this case, both 't is F' and 's is G' would be true, in which case 't is F and s is G' should also be true – which is not what (#1) entails.

The solution to this problem is straightforward. The truthmaker for a sentence of the form 'p and q' should be a *compound* fact, composed of a truthmaker for 'p' and a truthmaker for 'q'. To ensure there are enough compound facts to serve as truthmakers, it suffices to posit the following fact formation principle:

(Summation Principle)   Necessarily, for any facts Φ and Ψ, there exists a compound fact $\Phi + \Psi$ composed of Φ and Ψ.

So, in particular, there exists a compound fact **Miami + Muir**, composed of **Miami** and **Muir**.

The final step of the solution is to modify (#1) as follows:

(Conjunctive Correspondence)   'p and q' corresponds to $\Phi =_{\mathrm{df}}$ there exist Ψ, Δ such that $\Phi = \Psi + \Delta$, 'p' corresponds to Ψ and 'q' corresponds to Δ.

Since 'Miami is humid' corresponds to **Miami** and 'The Muir Glacier is melting' corresponds to **Muir**, the analysis of correspondence for conjunctions entails that 'Miami is humid and the Muir Glacier is melting' corresponds to **Miami + Muir**.

In combination with the analysis of correspondence for atomic sentences and the summation principle, the analysis of correspondence for conjunctions entails the correspondence schema for conjunctions of atomic sentences. To take an arbitrary example, consider the sentence 'The Earth is round and Venice is sinking'. By the analysis of correspondence for conjunctions, 'The Earth is round and Venice is sinking' corresponds to a fact if and only if there exists a compound fact $\Psi + \Delta$ such that 'The Earth is round' corresponds to Ψ and 'Venice is sinking' corresponds to Δ. By the summation principle, $\Psi + \Delta$ exists if and only if both Ψ and Δ exist individually. It follows that 'The Earth is round and Venice is sinking' corresponds to a fact if and only if 'The Earth is round' corresponds to a fact and 'Venice is sinking' corresponds to a fact. By the analysis of correspondence for atomic sentences, 'The Earth is round' corresponds to a fact if and only if the Earth is round, and 'Venice is sinking' corresponds to a fact if and only if Venice is sinking. Hence, 'The Earth is round and Venice is sinking' corresponds to a fact if and only if the Earth is round and Venice is sinking.

As in the case of disjunctions of atomic sentences, the correspondence theory gives us an explanation of the T-schema for conjunctions of atomic sentences. The reason why 'The Earth is round and Venice is sinking' is true if and only if the Earth is round and Venice is sinking is that (i) truth *just is* correspondence and (ii) 'The Earth is round and Venice is sinking' corresponds to a fact if and only if the Earth is round and Venice is sinking.

2.1.2.2.4 Negations of Atomic Sentences   Again following the pattern of 'or', one might expect the analysis of correspondence for sentences formed by the connective 'not', which are known as *negations*, to be:

(#2)   'it is not the case that p' corresponds to $\Phi =_{df}$ 'p' fails to correspond to Φ.

The problem with (#2) is that, when combined with the summation principle, it will make a large number of contradictions true, where a contradiction is a sentence of the form 'p and not p'. For example, because 'Miami is humid' fails to correspond to Muir, (#2) entails 'Miami is not humid' corresponds to Muir. But then, the contradiction 'Miami is humid and Miami is not humid' corresponds to the compound fact Miami + Muir, and so is true. This is clearly an unacceptable result.

Here is one possible way of solving this problem. Suppose a person is presently wearing a yellow shirt. Consequently, their shirt is not blue. What fact makes it the case that their shirt is not blue? The obvious answer is: the fact describable as *their shirt being yellow*, since being yellow excludes being blue.

More generally, we might assume the following principle:

(Exclusion Principle)   Necessarily, if $x_1, \ldots, x_n$ fail to stand in relation R, then there exists some alternative relation R^* such that (i) $x_1, \ldots, x_n$ stand in relation R^* and (ii) it is impossible for some things to simultaneously stand in both R and R^*.

For example, because Frankie, the dog, lacks the property of *being asleep*, there exists an alternative property, in this case the property of *being awake*, such that (i) Frankie has the property of being awake and (ii) it is impossible to simultaneously be asleep and awake.

In combination with the exclusion principle, the following analysis of correspondence for negations of atomic sentences entails the correspondence schema for negations of atomic sentences:

(Negative Atomic Correspondence)   '$t_1, \ldots, t_n$ are not R-related' corresponds to $\Phi =_{df} \Phi$ cannot co-exist with a fact composed of the objects which $t_1, \ldots, t_n$ refer to (arranged in that order) and the property which R refers to.

To take an arbitrary example, consider the sentence 'Oxford is not foggy'. By the analysis of correspondence for negations of atomic sentences, 'Oxford is not foggy' corresponds to a fact if and only if there exists a fact which cannot co-exist with a fact composed of the object which 'Oxford' refers to and the property which 'is foggy' refers to. 'Oxford' refers to Oxford and 'is foggy' refers to the property of being foggy. Thus, 'Oxford is not foggy' corresponds to a fact if and only if there exists a fact which cannot co-exist with a fact composed of Oxford and the property of being foggy. By the exclusion principle and the nature of facts, such a fact exists if and only if Oxford lacks the property of being foggy. Consequently, 'Oxford is not foggy' corresponds to a fact if and only if Oxford is not foggy.

As in the case of disjunctions and conjunctions of atomic sentences, the correspondence theory explains the T-schema for negations of atomic sentences. The reason why 'Oxford is not foggy' is true if and only if Oxford is not foggy is that (i) truth *just is* correspondence and (ii) 'Oxford is not foggy' corresponds to a fact if and only if Oxford is not foggy.

2.2 MOTIVATION

The correspondence theory is motivated by two key hypotheses about truth: *meaning sensitivity* and *responsiveness*. According to meaning sensitivity, a sentence has its truth condition in virtue of its meaning, rather than in virtue of anything intrinsic to the sentence. According to responsiveness, the truth status of a sentence is determined by how reality is configured and not the other way around. In this section, we explain in more detail these two key hypotheses and explain why the correspondence theory supports them.

2.2.1 MEANING SENSITIVITY

As previously discussed, an essential feature of truth is that the truth of 'p' is materially equivalent to the condition that p – which, recall, means that in actual fact, either 'p' is true and p or 'p' is not true and it is not the case that p. For example, the truth of 'It is raining in London' is materially equivalent to the condition that it is raining in London, since in actual fact, either 'It is raining in London' is true and rain is falling in London, or 'It is raining in London' is not true and rain is not falling in London.

The question remains as to whether the material equivalence between the truth of '*p*' and the condition that *p* is a necessary connection holding in every possible word, or a contingent connection established by the particularities of the actual world.

The meaning sensitivity hypothesis asserts that every sentence '*p*' has its truth condition in virtue of its meaning. Consequently, since the meaning of '*p*' could have been different, the truth condition of '*p*' could also have been different. Consider, for example, the sentence 'London is larger than Paris'. In actual fact, the truth of 'London is larger than Paris' is materially equivalent to the condition that London is larger than Paris. However, according to the meaning sensitivity hypothesis, if 'larger' had instead meant *smaller*, then the truth of 'London is larger than Paris' would have instead been materially equivalent to the condition that London is smaller than Paris.

As we saw in the previous section, which fact a sentence corresponds to is ultimately determined by the meanings of the names and predicates it contains. For example, 'Chicago is windy' corresponds to the fact of Chicago being windy because the meaning of 'Chicago' is Chicago and the meaning of 'is windy' is the property of being windy. Consequently, the correspondence theory (in combination with the background theory of facts and correspondence) entails that truth is meaning sensitive. In particular, if the meaning of 'Chicago' changed, so that it no longer meant Chicago but instead meant Detroit, then the truth condition of 'Chicago is windy' would no longer be the condition that Chicago is windy. Instead, the truth condition of 'Chicago is windy' would be the condition that *Detroit* is windy.

2.2.2 RESPONSIVENESS

Suppose the condition that *p* is materially equivalent to the condition that *q*. This leaves open the question of which of these conditions – if either – is more fundamental: does whether *p* determine whether *q*, or does whether *q* determine whether *p*?

A famous example of this phenomenon is the *Euthyphro dilemma*. According to many theists, God commands us to perform exactly those actions that are morally right. Consequently, an action is morally right if and only if God commands it. However, this leaves open the following two competing hypotheses:

1. whether God commands an action determines whether it is morally right
2. whether an action is morally right determines whether God commands it.

According to the first hypothesis, God's commandments are the ultimate source of morality. Proponents of the first hypothesis therefore face the problem of explaining why it is that, say, God commands us not to steal, since there is no moral prohibition on stealing independent of what God commands.

By contrast, according to the second hypothesis, the ultimate source of morality is external to God's commandments. Proponents of the second hypothesis therefore have no problem explaining why it is that God commands us not to steal − God commands us not to steal because he is a perfectly good being who knows the moral law. Instead, proponents of the second hypothesis face the problem of explaining where morality comes from, if not from God.

A dilemma similar in structure to the Euthythro dilemma can be raised for truth. Although we know that 'p' is true if and only if p, this is consistent with the following two competing hypotheses:

1. whether p determines whether 'p' is true
2. whether 'p' is true determines whether p.

Consider, for example, the true sentence 'There are wild elephants in Africa'. According to the first hypothesis, 'There are wild elephants in Africa' is true *because* Africa contains wild elephants. Thus, on this view, the truth of 'There are wild elephants in Africa' is determined by part of an independently existing reality − the part consisting of wild elephants in Africa.

By contrast, according to the second hypothesis, Africa contains wild elephants *because* the sentence 'There are wild elephants in Africa' is true. Thus, on this view, the truth of 'There are wild elephants in Africa' somehow constructs the part of reality which consists of wild elephants in Africa.

The responsiveness hypothesis asserts that the truth status of every sentence '*p*' is determined by whether *p*. In particular, 'There are wild elephants in Africa' is true because Africa contains wild elephants, 'The Grand Canyon is beautiful' is true because the Grand Canyon is beautiful, and 'There are finitely many prime numbers' is *un*true because the prime numbers are infinite in number. Truth is responsive, in the sense that it is always responding to the state of an independently existing reality, and never involved in constructing part of that reality.[4]

According to the correspondence theory, a sentence is true *because* it corresponds to a fact. In particular, 'California contains wild bears' is true *because* it corresponds to the fact of California containing wild bears, 'New Orleans is humid' is true *because* it corresponds to the fact of New Orleans being humid and 'Mount Everest is taller than K2' is true *because* it corresponds to the fact of Mount Everest being taller than K2.

Likewise, according to the correspondence theory, a sentence is untrue *because* it fails to correspond to a fact. In particular, 'Scotland contains wild bears' is untrue *because* there does not exist a fact of Scotland containing wild bears, 'Denver is humid' is untrue *because* there does not exist a fact of Denver being humid and 'Ama Dablam is taller than K2' is untrue *because* there does not exist a fact of Ama Dablam being taller than K2.

In general, given the actual meaning of '*p*', whether '*p*' is true is determined by whether there exists a fact describable as *it being the case that p*. But whether there exists a fact describable as *it being the case that p* is determined by whether *p*. For example, there exists a fact of California containing wild bears *because* California contains wild bears, there exists a fact of New Orleans being humid *because* New Orleans is humid and there does not exist a fact of Ama Dablam being taller than K2 *because* Ama Dablam is not taller than K2. Consequently, the correspondence theory entails that truth is responsive.

2.3 ARGUMENT FOR THE CORRESPONDENCE ANSWER

In this section, we outline what we take to be the most compelling argument for the correspondence answer. Here is the argument:

(1) There can be no difference in the state of reality without a difference in which entities exist.

(2) If there can be no difference in the state of reality without a difference in which entities exist then facts exist.

(3) Facts exist. [From (1), (2)]

(4) Truth is meaning sensitive.

(5) Truth is responsive.

(6) If facts exist, truth is meaning sensitive and truth is responsive then truth consists in correspondence to the facts.

---

(7) Truth consists in correspondence to the facts. [From (3), (4), (5), (6)]

2.3.1 REASONS FOR BELIEVING THE PREMISES

In this section, we give some reasons to believe the premises of the argument for the correspondence theory.

2.3.1.1 Premise (1)

According to premise (1), if a super-intelligent being were given a laundry list of everything that exists – Mount Everest, Belgium, Jupiter, etc. – then in principle they would be able to know everything there is to know about the state of reality. They would be able to know the total amount of water in Lake Michigan, the total number of stars in the Milky Way galaxy and the average temperature on Earth.

In the philosophy literature, premise (1) is referred to as the principle that *truth supervenes on being* (TSB). TSB is usually taken to be a foundational principle, which does not admit of deeper justification. Despite lacking further justification, many philosophers find it extremely plausible that changing what exists is the only way to change how reality is.

2.3.1.2 Premise (2)

It is uncontroversial that an inventory of everything would settle *some* questions about the state of reality. Most obviously, it would settle questions about which entities exist, such as the question of whether God exists. It is much more controversial whether an inventory of reality would settle *all* possible questions.

Consider, for example, the question of whether Frankie the dog is presently in his bed. The only entities whose existence seems relevant to answering this question are Frankie and his bed. Yet just knowing that both Frankie and his bed exist is not enough to know whether Frankie is *in* his bed – for perhaps Frankie is on the sofa instead.

To handle questions such as whether Frankie in his bed, proponents of TSB generally fall back on the existence of facts. In particular, once we accept the existence of facts, we can settle the question of whether Frankie is in his bed by checking through the list of everything that exists to see whether it contains a fact describable as *Frankie being in his bed*. Similarly, to settle the question of whether Anika's left arm is raised, it suffices to check through the list of everything that exists to see whether it contains a fact describable as *Anika's left arm being raised*. And so on.

2.3.1.3 Premise (4)

According to premise (4), a sentence has its truth condition in virtue of its meaning. This seems to be part of common sense. For example, given the way we actually use language, the truth of 'London is larger than Paris' is materially equivalent to the condition that London is larger than Paris. However, if we changed the way we used language, so that 'larger' came to mean *smaller*, then common sense suggests the truth of 'London is larger than Paris' would thereby become materially equivalent to the condition that London is smaller than Paris.

According to premise (5), whether a sentence 'p' is true is determined by whether p, and not the other way around. Thus, the role of truth is to merely track, and never construct, reality.

Like the thesis that truth is meaning sensitive, the thesis that truth is responsive seems to be rooted in common sense. For example, according to common sense, we are interested in whether 'God exists' is true because we are interested in whether *God exists*; we are interested in whether 'There is extra-terrestrial life' is true because we are interested in whether *there is extra-terrestrial life*; and we are interested in whether 'Nuclear war will break out this century' is true because we are interested in whether *nuclear war will break out this century*. According to this way of thinking, truth merely reflects what is already there in reality.

We can argue for premise (6) as an inference to the best explanation. Supposing facts exist, the correspondence theory provides the best explanation of meaning sensitivity and responsiveness, while also offering an explanation of the T-schema. The correspondence theory provides the *best* explanation because it reduces truth to a simple and natural property: the property of corresponding to a fact.

2.4   EVALUATION

There are two items to evaluate: the argument for the correspondence answer and the correspondence answer itself.

2.4.1   EVALUATION OF THE ARGUMENT

We find premises (2) and (6) to be beyond rebuke. However, premises (1), (4), and (5) are all open to question.

In our view, the weakest premise of the argument is premise (1), the principle that truth supervenes on being (TSB), because it is hard to find any further justification for it. Consequently, the argument will not be persuasive to those readers who do not find TSB to be self-evident.

But not only does TSB lack deeper justification, it also faces a wide array of plausible counterexamples: possibilities which appear to differ over how reality is without also differing over what exists. The plausible counterexamples to TSB are exactly those cases where proponents of TSB are forced to resort to facts to support their position. For example, take two possibilities which differ only in so far as in one, Frankie the dog is in his bed, but in the other, Frankie is on the sofa. Both possibilities, we suppose, agree on which ordinary objects exist (Frankie, his bed, the sofa, their various parts, and so on). Consequently, TSB can only be maintained at the cost of accepting the existence of additional, unordinary entities (facts), which can make the difference between these two possibilities. For many, this is reason enough to reject TSB all together.

2.4.1.2 Premise (4)

Although meaning sensitivity is part of our common sense conception of truth, meaning sensitivity also prevents truth from performing certain useful functions.

Consider, for example, the sentence K = 'King John agreed to the Magna Carta'. A historian, in the course of arguing that the signing of the Magna Carta ultimately caused the industrial revolution, might assert:

(C1) If K were not true then the industrial revolution would not have started in Britain.

The historian *intends* to use (C1) as a convenient shorthand for the following, more long-winded, statement:

(C2) If King John had not agreed to the Magna Carta then the industrial revolution would not have started in Britain.

However, given meaning sensitivity, (C1) and (C2) are not necessarily equivalent.

To see why, note that, given meaning sensitivity, K could fail to be true for two different reasons: the relevant facts could be different, or its meaning could be different. So a counterfactual scenario in which K is untrue is not automatically a scenario in which King John did not agree to the Magna Carta. For example, it is possible that if K were not true then King John would still have agreed to the Magna Carta, but 'agreed to' would have instead meant *not agreed to* − in which case K fails to be true because its meaning is different, rather than because the relevant facts are different. Since the relevant facts remain unchanged, the industrial revolution would still have started in Britain, thereby making (C1) false but (C2) true.

2.4.1.3 Premise (5)

Although in many cases it is part of common sense that whether 'p' is true is determined by whether p, and not the other way around, it is not clear that this goes for *all* cases. Consider, for example, the sentence 'The Grand Canyon is beautiful'. Plausibly, the Grand Canyon is beautiful not because of its intrinsic physical structure, but rather because of how humans respond to it. According to this way of thinking, humans *project* beauty onto the Grand Canyon, because the appearance of the Grand Canyon appeals to them. Beauty is not an objective property, like shape, which humans passively perceive.

Supposing this understanding of beauty is correct, we can now ask: how is it that humans manage to construct the fact of the Grand Canyon being beautiful? One interesting suggestion, which we explore in more detail in the chapter on the verifiability answer, is that the Grand Canyon is beautiful *because* the sentence 'The Grand Canyon is beautiful' is true. In turn, 'The Grand Canyon is beautiful' is true because it passes the test for truth established by humans. This test might include the requirement that the referent of 'The Grand Canyon' has a certain kind of shape, or a certain kind of color, which humans consider aesthetically appealing. But if this is right then responsiveness fails: truth does not merely respond to reality, but is also involved in constructing parts of reality.

2.4.2 EVALUATION OF THE ANSWER

In this subsection we outline three objections to the correspondence answer itself, which apply regardless of the argument used in support of it.

2.4.2.1 Weirdness

The most important objection to the correspondence theory is simply that facts are *weird*. Although we are used to thinking that ordinary material objects – such as bricks, wooden beams and body parts – can form larger wholes, the idea that an ordinary material object, such as a basketball, and an abstract property, such as roundness, could form a larger whole is highly peculiar.

Consider, for example, a fact **Basketball** composed of a particular basketball and the abstract property of roundness. If **Basketball** really exists, then presumably it is located somewhere. So where is it? The only viable answer appears to be: **Basketball** is located in the same place as the basketball. But if **Basketball** is located in the same place as the basketball then presumably all of **Basketball's** parts are located in the same place as the basketball. In particular, the abstract property of roundness is located in the same place as the basketball. However, this just does not seem right. For no matter how closely we inspect the basketball, we will never locate such a thing as the abstract property of roundness. Therefore, the proponent of facts faces an unpleasant dilemma: either **Basketball** is not located anywhere at all, or **Basketball** is not located where all of its parts are.

2.4.2.1.1 A Possible Reply The observation that a class of theoretical entities are weird is not by itself a sufficient reason to rule out their existence. For example, few think we should rule out the existence of quantum mechanical particles because they behave in weird ways. On the contrary, we *should* believe in quantum mechanical particles, because, in spite of their weirdness, the theory which requires their existence has proved remarkably successful at explaining and predicting experimental outcomes. Likewise, if the correspondence theory turns out to be the best theory of truth – the theory which best explains the phenomena associated with truth (primarily, the T-schema) – then we should believe in facts.

2.4.2.2 Truths about the Past

Let us grant, for the sake of argument, that facts about presently existing macroscopic phenomena really exist. When the basketball is round, there really does exist a fact composed of the basketball and the property of roundness. When Miami is humid, there really does exist a fact composed of Miami and humidity. When Mount Etna erupts, there really does exist a fact composed of Mount Etna and the property of erupting. Even granting this assumption, there remain categories of truths for which it is difficult to find corresponding facts.

One important category consists of truths about the past. In ordinary life, there are many sentences of the form 't is F' such that we take 'In the past it was the case that t is F' to be true while taking 't is F' to be untrue. Examples include: 'In the past, Henry VIII was a king', 'In the past, Chicago was a small settlement', 'In the past, Canada was mostly covered by ice'.

This poses a problem for the correspondence theory. To take one example, because 'Chicago is a small settlement' is untrue, there does not exist a fact describable as *Chicago being a small settlement*. On the other hand, because 'In the past, Chicago was a small settlement' *is* true, it must correspond to a fact. But since no fact exists which is describable as *Chicago being a small settlement*, it is unclear what fact 'In the past, Chicago was a small settlement' could correspond to.

2.4.2.2.1 A Possible Reply   An initially promising response is that truths about the past correspond to facts about the presently existing evidence for those truths. In particular, 'In the past, Chicago was a small settlement' corresponds to the presently existing fact of the 1830 survey of Chicago depicting a small settlement. More generally: truths about past political institutions correspond to facts concerning surviving governmental records, truths about ancient civilizations correspond to facts concerning buried ruins, truths about dinosaurs correspond to facts concerning dinosaur fossils, and truths about the prehistoric climate correspond to facts concerning the geological record.

The main problem with taking truths about the past to correspond to historical evidence is the *problem of insufficient evidence*: there is not enough historical evidence to settle all questions about the past. Consider, for example, the particular moment of time $t = 2:11\text{pm}$ on 03/05/1537. Ordinarily, we would assume that either Henry VIII sneezed at t or Henry VIII did not sneeze at t. But then, by the T-schema, either 'Henry VIII sneezed at t' is true or 'Henry VIII did not sneeze at t' is true. Consequently, if truths about the past correspond to historical evidence then either there exists conclusive historical of Henry VIII sneezing at t or there exists conclusive historical evidence of Henry VIII not sneezing at t. Clearly, however, it is highly unlikely that such historical evidence exists.

2.4.2.2.1 Another Possible Reply An alternative response to the problem of finding truthmakers for truths about the past is to reject the assumption that the only facts in existence are the presently existing facts. According to this view, time is spread out like a vast tapestry, running from the distant past to distant future, and we only observe a single cross-section of the tapestry – the present moment. Our relation to inhabitants of the distant past, such as Henry VIII, is therefore akin to our relation to inhabitants of distant countries. Consequently, there really does exist a fact of Henry VIII, say, sneezing at 2:11pm on 03/05/1537 – but this fact is simply located in a different cross-section of the temporal continuum.[5]

2.4.2.3 Mathematical Truth

Consider a mathematical truth, such as '13 is a prime number'. According to the correspondence theory, this sentence is true because it corresponds to a portion of reality composed of the number 13 and the property of being prime. Thus, according to the correspondence theory, mathematical reality has an existence independent of the truths about that reality.

However, many philosophers have questioned whether reality really contains independently existing mathematical objects such as numbers. After all, the number 13 does not have a location in space and time – there is no particular place where we can go to locate the number 13. Thus, supposing space and time encompass the entirety of independently existing reality, the correspondence theory cannot be the correct account of mathematical truth.

2.4.2.3.1 A Possible Reply   The typical response to the problem of mathematical truth is to reject the assumption that space and time encompass the entirety of independently existing reality. According to this view, certain objects – in particular, *numbers* – exist independently entirely outside of spacetime. Thus, mathematical truths are made true by an independently existing mathematical realm which transcends space and time. This position is known in the philosophy literature as *mathematical platonism*, after the Ancient Greek philosopher Plato, who first defended such a view.

An important challenge to mathematical platonism is the problem of explaining why we are justified in believing certain mathematical claims – such as '13 is a prime number' – are true. This challenge can be made clear by considering an analogous challenge for truths about ordinary macroscopic reality.

Consider, for example, our belief expressed by 'Paris is the capital of France'. Why are we justified in holding this belief? In this case, answering the challenge is not particularly hard: the belief 'Paris is the capital of France' is justified because it is, in a certain sense, *causally sustained* by the very fact that Paris is the capital of France.

First, after the government of France decided to make Paris the capital of France – thereby bringing the fact of Paris being the capital of France into existence – they communicated this to others around the world, who recorded the fact in various texts. These texts in turn eventually caused us to form the belief that Paris is the capital of France – either directly or indirectly, via a teacher, for example. Thus, the fact that Paris is the capital of France ultimately caused us to have the belief that Paris is the capital of France.

Second, if the government of France decided to change the capital to, for example, Marseille, then they would announce this publicly to the world. Supposing we pay some small amount of attention to current affairs – by browsing the internet or reading the newspaper – this announcement would ultimately cause us to drop our belief that Paris is the capital of France.

So our belief that Paris is the capital of France is justified because (a) the fact that Paris is the capital of France caused us to believe that Paris is the capital of France in the first place and (b) if the fact that Paris is the capital of France ceased to exist then we would cease to believe that Paris is the capital of France.

Generalizing from this example, the following general conditions on justified belief are plausible:

(Causal Justification)   A belief expressed by '*p*' is justified if and only if (a) the fact that *p* initially caused the belief and (b) if the fact that *p* ceased to exist then the belief would also cease to exist.

The problem for mathematical platonism is that, assuming mathematical platonism is true, neither (a) nor (b) holds when '*p*' is a mathematical truth. Consider, for example, our belief expressed by '13 is a prime number'. If the fact that 13 is a prime number exists independently outside of spacetime then it could not have had any causal impact on our brain at all – and so could not be the causal explanation for why we hold this belief. Similarly, if the fact that 13 is a prime number ceased to exist then, since it exists independently outside of spacetime, it would have no causal impact on our brain – and so we would continue to hold the belief.

Mathematical platonists must, therefore, provide an alternative, independently motivated account of justification – one which is compatible with the truthmaker for a justified belief being causally isolated from that belief. This is a substantial challenge, and it is unclear whether attempts by mathematical platonists to answer the challenge have been successful. For an in-depth discussion of the case for and against mathematical platonism, see Mark Balaguer, *Platonism and Anti-Platonism in Mathematics* (Oxford, 1998).

2.5 CHAPTER SUMMARY

In this chapter, we introduced the correspondence theory of truth, according to which truth consists in correspondence to the facts. We clarified the nature of the category of facts and the relation of correspondence. We then introduced the key notions of meaning sensitivity and responsiveness, and presented an argument for the correspondence theory on the basis that the theory entails truth is meaning sensitive, responsive and satisfies the T-schema. We surveyed some objections to this argument and to the correspondence theory more generally – in particular, the objection that facts do not exist; the objection that, even if facts do exist, there are no facts about the past; and the objection that there are no mathematical facts.

NOTES

3. Advanced readers should consult Appendix B (page 157) for a more precise formulation of the material in this section.

4. For more discussion of the distinction between responsive and non-responsive theories of truth, see Douglas Edwards, *The Metaphysics of Truth* (Oxford University Press: Oxford, 2018).

5. For further discussion of this view, see Theodore Sider, *Four-Dimensionalism: An Ontology of Persistence and Time* (Oxford University Press: Oxford, 2003).

FURTHER READING

- Historical background: Bertrand Russell, 'Truth and Falsehood', in *The Problems of Philosophy* (Oxford University Press Inc: Oxford, 1997, pp. 119 –130).
- Classic work: Marian David, *Correspondence and Disquotation: An Essay on the Nature of Truth* (Oxford University Press: Oxford, 1994); David M. Armstrong, *Truth and Truthmakers* (Cambridge University Press: Cambridge, 2004).
- Contemporary discussion: Mark Jago, *What Truth Is* (Oxford University Press: Oxford, 2018).

SEMANTIC

3.1 ANSWER TO THE CENTRAL QUESTION

According to the semantic theory of truth, the meanings of the names and predicates in a sentence combine in a systematic way to determine the truth condition of the sentence. A sentence is then made true by its truth condition obtaining.

So far, the semantic theory is indistinguishable from the correspondence theory. The innovation of the semantic theory is that it does not reduce truth to a property involving facts. Instead, the semantic theory reduces truth to a property we call *semantic correctness*, which is definable without reference to any philosophically controversial entities:

(Semantic Theory) x is true $=_{df} x$ is semantically correct.

The remainder of this section is dedicated to the definition of semantic correctness.

3.1.1 INDUCTIVE DEFINITIONS

The definition of semantic correctness is a type of definition known as an *inductive* definition. As an example of an inductive definition,

DOI: 10.4324/9781003190103-3

consider the property of being a descendant of Genghis Khan. This property is defined as follows:

(Descendant of GK) x is a descendant of Genghis Khan $=_{df}$ x is a child of Genghis Khan or x is the child of a descendant of Genghis Khan.

Note that the property this definition is attempting to define – *being a descendant of Genghis Khan* – occurs in the definition. The definition is therefore circular. However, we should distinguish two ways in which a definition can be circular.

The first kind of circularity, known as *vicious* circularity, occurs when the definition fails to determine whether the defined property applies in particular cases. As an example of a viciously circular definition, consider

(Viciously Circular) x is blue $=_{df}$ x is blue.

This definition does not allow us to determine whether a given object is blue, since to do so we would already need to know whether the object is blue. Viciously circular definitions are therefore defective.

By contrast, the second kind of circularity, known as *virtuous* circularity, occurs when the definition *does* determine whether the defined property applies in particular cases. The definition of being a descendant of Genghis Kahn is an example of a virtuously circular definition. To see why, consider a given person x. To determine whether x is a descendant of Genghis Khan, it suffices to check whether there exists a sequence of people $y_1, y_2, y_3, \ldots, y_n$ such that (i) y_1 is a child of Genghis Khan, (ii) y_n is x and (iii) for every $i < n$, y_i is a parent of y_{i+1}. If so, we know x is a descendant of Genghis Khan. If not, we know x is not.

In general, an inductive definition defines a property P by first defining, in an entirely non-circular manner, an initial set of objects with property P, and then specifies rules by which P can be transferred from one object to another. For example, in the case of being a descendant of Genghis Khan, the definition first specifies that the children of Genghis Khan are descendants, and then specifies that a descendant transfers the property of being a descendant to their children. Inductive definitions are virtuously circular because, to decide whether a given object x has an inductively defined property P, it suffices to check whether x can be obtained by repeatedly applying the transfer rules to some objects in the initial set.[6]

3.1.2 SEMANTIC CORRECTNESS

We now turn to the definition of semantic correctness. For simplicity, we define semantic correctness for the fragment of English obtained by repeatedly applying the connectives 'and', 'or' and 'not' to atomic sentences. Note, however, that a fully general definition of semantic correctness would need to apply to *all* complex sentences.

3.1.2.1 Base Cases

In accordance with the structure of an inductive definition, we begin by defining, in an entirely non-circular manner, which atomic sentences and negations of atomic sentences are semantically correct. These definitions are known as the *base cases* of the definition of semantic correctness.

(Positive Base Case)   '$t_1,...,t_n$ are R-related' is semantically correct $=_{df}$ the objects referred to by $t_1,...,t_n$ (in that order) stand in the relation referred to by R.

(Negative Base Case)   '$t_1,...,t_n$ are not R-related' is semantically correct $=_{df}$ the objects referred to by $t_1,...,t_n$ (in that order) do not stand in the relation referred to by R.

For example, 'The Amazon is shrinking' is semantically correct because the object referred to by 'The Amazon' has the property referred to by 'is shrinking'. Similarly, 'Monaco is not colder than Scotland' is semantically correct because the objects referred to by 'Monaco' and 'Scotland', in that order, do not stand in the relation referred to by 'is colder than'.

Our background knowledge entails that an atomic sentence 'p' is semantically correct if and only if p. Consequently, analyzing truth as semantic correctness explains the T-schema for atomic sentences. To take an arbitrary example, consider the sentence 'The Pacific Ocean is frozen over'. This sentence is formed by applying 'is frozen over' to 'The Pacific Ocean'. Thus, 'The Pacific Ocean is frozen over' is semantically correct if and only if the object referred to by 'The Pacific Ocean' has the property referred to by 'is frozen over'. We know that 'The Pacific Ocean' refers to the Pacific Ocean and 'is frozen over' refers to the property of being frozen over. Consequently, 'The Pacific Ocean is frozen over' is semantically correct if and only if the Pacific Ocean is frozen over.

Likewise, our background knowledge entails that the negation 'not p' of an atomic sentence 'p' is semantically correct if and only if it is not the case that p. Consequently, analyzing truth as semantic correctness also explains the T-schema for negations of atomic sentences. To take an arbitrary example, consider the sentence 'Oxford is not foggy'. This sentence is formed by applying 'is foggy' to 'Oxford'. Thus, 'Oxford is not foggy' is semantically correct if and only if the object referred to by 'Oxford' lacks the property referred to by 'is foggy'. We know that 'Oxford' refers to Oxford and 'is foggy' refers to the property of being foggy. Consequently, 'Oxford is not foggy' is semantically correct if and only if Oxford is not foggy.

3.1.2.2 Inductive Clauses

Next, we specify the rules by which semantic correctness is passed from one sentence to another. More specifically, we reduce the question of whether an un-negated complex sentence (a complex sentence without 'not' at the front) is semantically correct to the question of whether its constituents are semantically correct. Similarly, we reduce the question of whether a negated complex sentence (a complex sentence *with* 'not' at the front) is semantically correct to the question of whether the negations of its constituents are semantically correct. These rule are known as the *inductive clauses* of the definition of semantic correctness.

1. 'p and q' is semantically correct $=_{df}$ both of 'p', 'q' are semantically correct.
2. 'p or q' is semantically correct $=_{df}$ at least one of 'p', 'q' is semantically correct.

3. 'not not p' is semantically correct $=_{df}$ 'p' is semantically correct.
4. 'not (p and q)' is semantically correct $=_{df}$ at least one of 'not p', 'not q' is semantically correct.
5. 'not (p or q)' is semantically correct $=_{df}$ both of 'not p', 'not q' are semantically correct.

Consider, for example, sentence

(S) Neptune is blue, and it is not the case that either Mars is blue or Jupiter is blue.

It follows from the base cases and inductive clauses that (S) is semantically correct. First, by the negative base case, 'Mars is not blue' and 'Jupiter is not blue' are semantically correct. Thus, by inductive clause 5, 'it is not the case that either Mars is blue or Jupiter is blue' is semantically correct. Also, by the positive base case, 'Neptune is blue' is semantically correct. Consequently, by inductive clause 1, (S) is semantically correct.

We now show that if 'p' and 'q' are atomic sentences then

(i) 'p and q' is semantically correct if and only if p and q
(ii) 'p or q' is semantically correct if and only if p or q.

Thus, like the correspondence theory, the semantic theory explains the T-schema for conjunctions and disjunctions of atomic sentences, in addition to atomic sentences and their negations.

3.1.2.2.1 Conjunctions of Atomic Sentences

To take an arbitrary example, consider the sentence 'The Earth is round and Venice is sinking'. 'The Earth is round and Venice is sinking' is semantically correct if and only if 'The Earth is round' is semantically correct and 'Venice is sinking' is semantically correct. By the positive base case, 'The Earth is round' is semantically correct if and only if the Earth is round, and 'Venice is sinking' is semantically correct if and only if Venice is sinking. Consequently 'The Earth is round and Venice is sinking' is semantically correct if and only if the Earth is round and Venice is sinking.

3.1.2.2.2 Disjunctions of Atomic Sentences   To take an arbitrary example, consider the sentence 'Chicago is windy or London is windy'. 'Chicago is windy or London is windy' is semantically correct if and only if 'Chicago is windy' is semantically correct or 'London is windy' is semantically correct. By the positive base case, 'Chicago is windy' is semantically correct if and only if Chicago is windy, and 'London is windy' is semantically correct if and only if London is windy. Consequently, 'Chicago is windy or London is windy' is semantically correct if and only if Chicago is windy or London is windy.

3.2   MOTIVATION

In the previous chapter, we observed that the correspondence theory has three nice features:

1. The correspondence theory explains the T-schema.
2. The correspondence theory entails that truth is meaning sensitive (i.e., the correspondence theory entails that if a sentence had meant something different then it would have had a different truth condition).
3. The correspondence theory entails that truth is responsive (i.e., the correspondence theory entails that truth is determined by how reality is configured, and not the other way around).

These three features are nice because the T-schema, meaning sensitivity and responsiveness collectively constitute our common sense conception of truth.

However, we observed that the benefits of the correspondence theory come at the cost of accepting the existence of *facts*, which form an unusual category of theoretical entity. For example, according to the theory of facts, for the dog to be in his bed there must exist three entities: the dog, the dog's bed and, in addition (this is the controversial part), *the fact of the dog being in his bed*, which is a structured entity composed of the dog, the dog's bed and the abstract relation of containment.

Many philosophers are skeptical that facts exist. Consequently, it is desirable to find an analysis of truth which has the three nice features outlined above, but which is not committed to the existence of facts. The semantic theory is one example of such an analysis. We have already seen that the semantic theory explains the T-schema. In the remainder of this section, we explain why the semantic theory entails meaning sensitivity and responsiveness.

3.2.1 MEANING SENSITIVITY

According to the semantic theory, the truth condition of an atomic sentence is determined by which entities the names and predicates in the sentence refer to. For example, the truth condition of 'London is larger than Paris' is the condition that London is larger than Paris because 'London' refers to London, 'Paris' refers to Paris and 'is larger than' refers to the relation of being larger than. Consequently, if 'larger' had instead meant *smaller* then, according to the semantic theory, the truth condition of 'London is larger than Paris' would have instead been the condition that London is smaller than Paris. Therefore, the semantic theory entails that truth for atomic sentences is meaning sensitive – and a similar argument shows the same for negations of atomic sentences.

By the definition of semantic correctness, the observation that truth for atomic sentences and their negations is meaning sensitive entails that truth for any complex sentence formed by repeatedly applying 'and', 'or' and 'not' to atomic sentences is meaning sensitive. Consider, for example, the complex sentence 'London is larger than Paris and Paris is larger than Florence'. According to the semantic theory, the truth condition of this sentence is the conjunction of the truth conditions of the atomic sentences 'London is larger than Paris' and 'Paris is larger than Florence'. Thus, since truth for atomic sentences is meaning sensitive, the truth of 'London is larger than Paris and Paris is larger than Florence' is also meaning sensitive.

3.2.2 RESPONSIVENESS

Consider the atomic sentence 'Neptune is blue'. According to the semantic theory, 'Neptune is blue' is true because

(i) 'Neptune is blue' is formed by applying 'is blue' to 'Neptune'
(ii) 'Neptune' refers to Neptune and 'is blue' refers to the property of being blue
(iii) Neptune has the property of being blue.

Since Neptune has the property of being blue *because* Neptune is blue, 'Neptune is blue' is true because Neptune is blue.

On the other hand, consider the atomic sentence 'Mars is blue'. According to the semantic theory, 'Mars is blue' is *not* true because

(i) 'Mars is blue' is formed by applying 'is blue' to 'Mars'
(ii) 'Mars' refers to Mars and 'is blue' refers to the property of being blue
(iii) Mars lacks the property of being blue.

Since Mars lacks the property of being blue *because* Mars is not blue, 'Mars is blue' fails to be true because Mars is not blue.

These observations generalize to all other atomic sentences. In general, given the actual meaning of '$t_1, \ldots, t_n$ are R-related', the semantic theory entails that the truth status of '$t_1, \ldots, t_n$ are R-related' is determined by whether $t_1, \ldots, t_n$ are R-related. In particular, 'Scotland is colder than Monaco' is true because Scotland is colder than Monaco, 'Venice is sinking' is true because Venice is sinking and 'Raleigh is closer to New York than to Washington DC' is *not* true because Raleigh is not closer to New York than to Washington DC. Therefore, according to the semantic theory, truth for atomic sentences is responsive – and a similar argument shows that truth for negations of atomic sentences is also responsive.

As in the case of meaning sensitivity, the definition of semantic correctness ensures the responsiveness of atomic sentences and their negations is transmitted to any complex sentence formed by repeatedly applying 'and', 'or' and 'not' to atomic sentences. Consider, for example, the complex truth 'The Earth is round and Venice is sinking'. By the semantic theory, 'The Earth is round and Venice is sinking' is true *because* 'The Earth is round' is true and 'Venice is sinking' is true. Since atomic truth is responsive, 'The Earth is round' is true *because* the Earth is round and 'Venice is sinking' is true *because* Venice is sinking. Therefore 'The Earth is round and Venice is sinking' is true *because* the Earth is round and Venice is sinking.

3.3 ARGUMENT FOR THE SEMANTIC ANSWER

We now turn to the question of how to argue for the semantic answer to the central question. Our motivation for investigating the semantic theory was the desire to find an analysis of truth which entails truth is meaning sensitive and responsive, but which is not committed to the existence of facts. This motivation provides what we consider to be the central argument for the semantic answer:

(1) Truth is meaning sensitive.
(2) Truth is responsive.
(3) Facts do not exist.
(4) If truth is meaning sensitive, truth is responsive and facts do not exist then truth is semantic correctness.

---

(5) Truth is semantic correctness. [From (1), (2), (3), (4)]

3.3.1 REASONS FOR BELIEVING THE PREMISES

3.3.1.1 Premises (1) and (2)

As discussed in Sections 2.2.1 and 2.2.2, meaning sensitivity and responsiveness form part of our common sense conception of truth. This entails premises (1) and (2), by default, have a high degree of plausibility, which can only be undermined by compelling reasons for disbelieving them.

3.3.1.2 Premise (3)

As discussed in Section 2.4.2.1, facts are *weird*. Whereas we are used to the idea that ordinary material objects, like biological cells, wooden planks and bricks, can compose larger entities, the idea that material objects, like Mount Everest and K2, and abstract relations, like *being taller than*, can compose larger entities is peculiar. Consequently, the existence of facts is, on its face, implausible.

3.3.1.3 Premise (4)

We can argue for premise (4) as an inference to the best explanation. To our knowledge, the semantic theory is the *only* known analysis of truth which is consistent with the non-existence of facts, provides an explanation of the T-schema and entails that truth is both meaning sensitive and responsive. Thus, the semantic theory currently provides the best explanation of the T-schema, meaning sensitivity and responsiveness under the assumption that facts do not exist.

3.4 EVALUATION

There are two items to evaluate: the central argument for the semantic answer and the semantic answer itself.

3.4.1 EVALUATION OF THE ARGUMENT

Although premise (4) is highly plausible given our present state of knowledge, premises (1), (2) and (3) are all open to question.

3.4.1.1 Premise (1)

In Section 2.4.1.2 we explained one reason to be skeptical of meaning sensitivity. In brief: meaning sensitivity is doubtful because some of the ways we would like to utilize the truth predicate require the truth of 'p' to be necessarily equivalent to the condition that p.

3.4.1.2 Premise (2)

In Section 2.4.1.3 we explained one reason to be skeptical of responsiveness. In brief: responsiveness is doubtful because there are some conditions, such as the condition that the Grand Canyon is beautiful, which seem to obtain because of how we respond to reality, rather than because of how reality is in itself. In these cases, truth is plausibly involved in constructing the relevant part of reality, rather than merely responding to reality.

3.4.1.3 Premise (3)

In Section 2.3.1.1 we saw the existence of facts can be motivated by the principle that *truth supervenes on being* (TSB), according to which there can be no difference in the state of reality without a difference in which entities exist. Facts are needed to support TSB due to the existence of possible situations which differ over how reality is but contain all the same ordinary objects. Consider, for example, a possible situation in which the mug is on the desk and a possible situation in which the mug is under the desk. Both possibilities agree on which ordinary objects exist (the mug, the desk and their various parts). Therefore, the proponent of TSB needs to posit the existence of *un*ordinary entities — namely, the fact of the mug being on the desk and the fact of the mug being under the desk — to make a difference between these possibilities.

3.4.2 EVALUATION OF THE ANSWER

In this section, we consider three objections to the semantic answer, which apply regardless of the argument used in support of it.

3.4.2.1 Generalizing Semantic Correctness

We showed how to define semantic correctness only for a restricted fragment of English – the part obtained by repeatedly applying the connectives 'and', 'or' and 'not' to atomic sentences. Thus, for the semantic theory to offer a complete account of truth for English, the definition of semantic correctness would need to be generalized to cover sentence formed using other kinds of connectives, such as *quantifiers* ('every', 'at least one'), *modal operators* ('necessarily', 'possibly'), *propositional attitudes* ('Jane believes that', 'Kevin hopes that') and *explanatory connectives* ('because', 'in virtue of'). Some progress has been made on this problem. In particular, Tarski showed how to define truth in a semantic style for quantifiers and Kripke showed how to define truth in a semantic style for modal operators.[7] Despite this progress, it remains controversial how to define truth in a semantic style for sentences containing propositional attitudes and explanatory connectives.

3.4.2.1.1 A Possible Reply   A proponent of the semantic theory may respond that the theory is presently a *work in progress*, and point to the successes of Tarski and Kripke as evidence the theory will eventually be extended to cover all of English. Furthermore, there *have* been proposals for how to semantically define truth for sentences containing propositional attitudes and explanatory connectives, which

some linguists and philosophers find compelling, though these proposals have not yet achieved the same level of consensus as Tarski and
Kripke.[8]

3.4.2.2 Wittgenstein's Paradox

The semantic theory requires that, in a given context of use, every
name refers to a unique object and every n-place predicate refers to
a unique n-place relation.[9] For example, according to the semantic
theory, 'Paris is in France' is true because (i) 'Paris' uniquely refers
to Paris, (ii) 'France' uniquely refers to France, (iii) 'is in' uniquely
refers to the 2-place relation of being located in and (iv) Paris and
France, in that order, stand in the relation of being located in.

These referential links between language and the world are
assumed by the semantic theory to be part of the meaning of English.
Consequently, whether a particular name refers to a particular object
or a particular n-place predicate refers to a particular n-place relation
is largely determined by the manner in which speakers of English
happen to use language. For example, given this understanding of
reference, 'Paris' refers to Paris not because of anything intrinsic
to the sequence of symbols P-a-r-i-s, but rather because of a long-
established linguistic convention, one that could have been different.
And if it had been different, 'Paris' might have instead referred to
Berlin, thereby giving 'Paris is in France' the truth condition that
Berlin is in France.

Wittgenstein's paradox, originally due to Ludwig Wittengstein and
later elaborated by Saul Kripke, calls into question the possibility of
giving a plausible account of how the linguistic behavior of speakers
determines, in a given context of use, a unique assignment of names
and predicates to entities in the world.[10] If no such account can be
given then it is doubtful whether the kind of language-world links
required by the semantic theory really exist. In this section, we briefly
outline Wittgenstein's paradox and sketch one possible solution.

3.4.2.2.1 The Paradox Consider the monadic predicate 'is a
human'. According to common sense, this predicate has, in the
recent past, always referred to the property of being a human. Suppose a skeptic challenges this common sense view by suggesting that,
although 'is a human' *now* refers to the property of being a human,

prior to the present moment 'is a human' instead referred to the property of being one of the first 200 billion humans to ever live (call this alternative property *the property of being an early human*). Thus, according to the skeptic, yesterday everyone using the word 'human' actually meant *early human*. How can we refute the skeptic's bizarre hypothesis?

To refute the skeptic, we need to identify the aspect of our past use of the predicate 'is a human' which ensured it referred to the property of being a human, rather than to the property of being an early human. Wittgenstein's paradox is essentially the observation that refuting the skeptic is a far more difficult task than we might naively suppose.

The significance of this is as follows. If the skeptic cannot be refuted, then it is false that 'is a human' previously singled out the property of being a human. But since there are no relevant differences between 'is a human' and other predicates, it would follow that *none* of our predicates previously singled out any properties or relations in particular. Consequently, since there are no relevant differences between our past use of language and our present use of language, none of our predicates *right now* single out any properties or relations in particular, and so the referential relations posited by the semantic theory simply do not exist.

We now discuss some possible ways of responding to the skeptic. As a first attempt, we might say that, prior to the present moment, 'is a human' referred to the property of being a human because speakers of English only ever applied 'is a human' to humans and only ever disapplied 'is a human' to non-humans (a speaker disapplies a monadic predicate to an object when the speaker describes the object as failing to satisfy the predicate). There are two main problems with this account.

First, it is not actually the case that speakers have only ever applied 'is a human' to humans and disapplied 'is a human' to non-humans. For example, there have surely been occasions where a speaker accidentally applied 'is a human' to a manakin dressed as a human, or disapplied 'is a human' to a human in costume.

Second, more importantly, since fewer than 200 billion humans have ever lived, whenever a speaker in the past applied 'is a human' to a human, they also applied 'is a human' to an *early* human. In addition, since every early human is also a human, whenever a speaker disapplied 'is a human' to a non-human, they also disapplied 'is a human' to a non-early-human. Consequently, our first response to the skeptic is equally compatible with the skeptic's hypothesis that, prior to the present moment, 'is a human' referred to the property of being an early human.

It is likely you did not find our first attempt at refuting the skeptic very compelling. This is because, ordinarily, we would say that a child has learned the meaning of 'is a human' not when they have memorized a finite list of entities to which 'is a human' has previously been applied or disapplied, but rather when they have internalized a rule for using 'is a human'. It is this rule – not a finite list of examples – which enables the child to competently apply 'is a human' to new cases.

Consequently, a more plausible response to the skeptic is that, prior to the present moment, 'is a human' referred to the property of being a human because *correctly* following the established rule for using 'is a human' could only ever result in 'is a human' being applied to humans. In particular, 'is a human' did not refer to the property of being an early human because the rule for using 'is a human' allows it to be applied to humans born after the early humans.

The problem with this account – and here lies the real bite of Wittgenstein's paradox – is that the rules for using language are themselves expressed in language. Consequently, just as the skeptic posits a bizarre interpretation of 'is a human', they could posit an equally bizarre interpretation of the rule for using 'is a human'.

Suppose, for example, that the following rule for using 'is a human' is suggested:

(Rule For Using 'is a human')   Apply 'is a human' to an entity if and only if the entity belongs to the same species as us.

The skeptic might respond that, although 'is a species' *now* refers to the property of being a species, prior to the present moment 'is a species' instead referred to the property of being the initial segment of a species consisting of the first 200 billion members. Thus, the rule for using 'is a human' is compatible with the skeptic's original hypothesis that, prior to the present moment, 'is a human' referred to the property of being an early human.

The proponent of the rule-based solution might respond by giving a rule for using 'is a species' which excludes the skeptic's deviant interpretation. For instance:

(Rule For Using 'is a species')   Apply 'is a species' to an entity if and only if the entity is a natural population of interbreeding organisms which is reproductively isolated from other such populations.[11]

But now the skeptic can simply assert that, although 'is a natural population' *now* refers to the property of being a natural population, prior to the present moment 'is a natural population' instead referred to the property of being the initial segment of a natural population consisting of the first 200 billion members. So, once again, the rule-based solution is made consistent with the skeptic's deviant interpretation of 'is a human'.

The proponent of the rule-based solution could go on to give a further rule for using 'is a natural population', but the skeptic will also be able to give a deviant interpretation of *that* rule which accords with their desired interpretation of 'is a human'. Clearly, this process can continue indefinitely. But nobody can internalize infinitely many rules. So eventually we will end up at a rule so basic that the meanings of the words in the rule cannot be fixed by any further rules. Once the skeptic gives a deviant interpretation of this basic rule (which they surely will be able to do), the proponent of the rule-based solution will have no recourse to additional rules to respond to the skeptic. Consequently, simply positing a collection of rules for using language is not enough to determine a unique meaning for 'is a human' – and so is not enough to determine a unique meaning for *any* of our predicates.

3.4.2.2.2 A Possible Reply   Although a full discussion of proposed solutions to Wittgenstein's paradox would take us beyond the scope of this book, we will briefly sketch one fairly popular solution, known as *reference magnetism*.[12]

Reconsider the initial proposal that, prior to the present moment, 'is a human' referred to the property of being a human because speakers of English only ever applied 'is a human' to humans and only ever disapplied 'is a human' to non-humans. The first problem with this account is that speakers sometimes misapply 'is a human'. Let us temporarily set this problem aside and suppose that speakers really have only ever applied 'is a human' to humans and disapplied 'is a human' to non-humans. There remains the problem that, since every previously existing human was also an early human, speakers have only ever applied 'is a human' to early humans and disapplied 'is a human' to non-early-humans. Thus, according to this account, the property of being an early human is an equally good candidate for the meaning of 'is a human'.

Here is a more precise characterization of the problem. Let H_A denote the set of entities to which speakers have previously applied 'is a human' and let H_D denote the set of entities to which speakers have previously disapplied 'is a human'. By our simplifying assumption, H_A contains only humans and H_D contains only non-humans. Despite this, there are still multiple properties which are shared by all members of H_A but not exemplified by any member of H_D – e.g., the property of being one of the first 200 billion humans, the property of being one of the first 201 billion humans, the property of being one of the first 202 billion humans, and so on. Thus, an account of reference which takes the referent of 'is a human' to be any property which is shared by all members of H_A but not exemplified by any member of H_D will fail to single out a unique referent for 'is a human'.

To fix this problem, an additional criterion is needed to filter out the unwanted properties. The theory of reference magnetism provides us with such a criterion. This theory builds on the observation that properties can be ordered according to their relative naturalness. For example, the property *being electrically charged* is more natural than the property *being electrically charged prior to 10.31am on 03/17/1994*. The reason why is that 10.31am on 03/17/1994 is an arbitrary cut-off point, which does not constitute a real joint in nature. Consequently, whereas the predicate 'is electrically charged' is highly likely to occur in a scientific textbook, the predicate 'was electrically charged prior to 10.31am on 03/17/1994' is highly unlikely to occur in a scientific textbook.

According to reference magnetism, the referent of 'is a human' is the *most natural* property which is shared by all members of H_A but not exemplified by any member of H_D. More generally, when we allow that 'is a human' may have been misused (so that H_A contains some non-humans and H_D contains some humans), reference magnetism takes the referent of 'is a human' to be the most natural property which *best fits* the way speakers have historically applied and disapplied 'is a human'.

It is plausible that the property of being a human is in fact the most natural property which best fits the way speakers have historically applied and disapplied 'is a human'. In particular, although the property of being an early human is equally fitting, it is much less natural than the property of being a human, since, to the best of our knowledge, nothing special distinguishes the early humans from later humans – and so the number 200 billion is an arbitrary cut-off point. Thus, reference magnetism plausibly entails that the property of being a human is the unique referent of 'is a human', thereby refuting the skeptic.

3.4.2.3 Fictional Characters

Consider the sentence 'Harry Potter is a wizard'. At first glance, this sentence is true – Harry Potter is indeed a wizard in the eponymous book series. Consequently, according to the semantic theory, 'Harry Potter is a wizard' is true because 'Harry Potter' refers to some independently existing object x, and x has the property of being a wizard. Clearly, however, wizards do not actually exist. Therefore, there is no object for 'Harry Potter' to refer to, and so the semantic theory cannot be right. This, in short, is the *fictional character objection* to the semantic theory.

3.4.2.3.1 A Possible Reply   The fictional character objection, as it stands, has a straightforward response. Although the sentence 'In the Harry Potter book series, Harry Potter is a wizard' is unquestionably true, it does not follow from this that the sentence 'Harry Potter is a wizard' is true. Compare: although 'In *The Man in the High Castle*, the Allies lost WW2' is true, 'The Allies lost WW2' is untrue. So what happens inside a novel can differ from what happens outside the novel. Consequently, proponents of the semantic theory can simply reject the assumption that 'Harry Potter is a wizard' is true. This sentence only seems true because it is true according to the novels.

3.4.2.3.2 A Stronger Objection   Although the initial version of the fictional character objection poses little threat to the semantic theory, there is a modified version of the fictional character objection which is much trickier to deal with. For even granting sentences about Harry Potter inside the novels are untrue, there remain seemingly true statements about Harry Potter which reside *outside* the novels. Most notably, the sentence 'Harry Potter is a fictional character' seems to be true. But then, according to the semantic theory, there independently exists an object x such that x has the property of being a fictional character and 'Harry Potter' refers to x. Unfortunately for the semantic theory, it is hard to see what kind of entity x could possibly be. After all, we do not ordinarily bump into fictional characters on the street.

Note that the response we gave to the initial fictional character objection does not carry over to the modified fictional character objection. This is because it is simply false that in the novels, Harry Potter is a fictional character. Rather, according to the novels, Harry Potter is a real flesh-and-blood wizard. Consequently, we cannot explain away the appearance that 'Harry Potter is a fictional character' is true on the basis that it is true according to the novels.

Therefore it appears the semantic theory *really is* committed to the independent existence of fictional characters. Whether this is palatable depends on whether a reasonable theory can be given as to the nature of these mysterious entities.[13]

3.5   CHAPTER SUMMARY

In this chapter, we introduced the semantic theory of truth, according to which truth consists in semantic correctness. We clarified the nature of semantic correctness and of inductively defined properties more generally. We then outlined an argument for the semantic theory on the basis that, like the correspondence theory, it entails that truth is meaning sensitive, responsive and satisfies the T-schema; but, unlike the correspondence theory, is not committed to the existence of facts. Finally, we discussed some objections to this argument and to the semantic theory more generally – in particular, the objection from Wittgenstein's paradox and the objection from fictional characters.

NOTES

6. An elementary mathematical technique can be used to formulate many inductive definitions in a non-circular manner. See Appendix C (page 159) for an application of this technique to the definition of semantic correctness.

7. The mechanics of Tarski's definition of truth – which applies to sentences containing quantifiers ('every', 'at least one') – can be found in any introductory logic textbook, such as Jc Beall and Shay Logan, *Logic: The Basics* (Routledge: New York, 2017). The mechanics of Kripke's definition of truth for sentences containing modal operators can be found in any introductory modal logic textbook, such as Jc Beall and Bas van Fraassen, *Possibilities and Paradox* (Oxford University Press: Oxford, 2003).

8. For a textbook-length introduction to the project of semantically defining truth for English, see Richard Larson and Gabriel Segal, *Knowledge and Meaning* (MIT Press: Cambridge, MA, 1995).

9. Recall from the discussion of context sensitivity in Section 1.3.9 that we assume a context of use has been implicitly fixed in the background.

10. Our discussion of Wittgenstein's paradox closely tracks Kripke's account of the paradox in his book *Wittgenstein on Rules and Private Language* (Wiley: Hoboken, NJ: 1984). It is controversial to what extent Kripke's interpretation of Wittgenstein is historically accurate. Wittgenstein's original discussion of the paradox can be found in his classic text *Philosophical Investigations* (Wiley-Blackwell: Hoboken, NJ, 2009). However, since *Philosophical Investigations* is notoriously difficult to understand, we recommend starting with Kripke's book.

11. This definition is from Ernst Mayr, *Systematics and the Origin of Species from the Viewpoint of a Zoologist* (Harvard University Press: Cambridge, MA, 1996).

12. The theory of reference magnetism is originally due to David Lewis, 'New Work for a Theory of Universals', *Australasian Journal of Philosophy*, Vol. 61, No. 4, pp. 343–377, 1983.

13. For more discussion of the fictional character objection and related issues, see Saul Kripke, *Reference and Existence* (Oxford University Press: Oxford, 2018).

FURTHER READING

- Historical background: Alfred Tarski, 'The Semantic Conception of Truth', *Philosophy and Phenomenological Research*, Vol. 4, No, 3, pp. 341–376, 1944.

- Classic work: Hartry Field, 'Tarski's Theory of Truth', *The Journal of Philosophy*, Vol. 69, No. 13, pp. 347–375, 1972.
- Contemporary discussion: Douglas Patterson (ed.), *New Essays on Tarski and Philosophy* (Oxford University Press: Oxford, 2008).

VERIFIABILITY

4.1 ANSWER TO THE CENTRAL QUESTION

The correspondence and semantic theories both agree on a core conception of truth as *responsive to the world*. According to these theories, each sentence is associated with a worldly condition and is made true by this condition obtaining.

Although this picture of truth is intuitively appealing when applied to sentences about ordinary macroscopic reality – the level of reality occupied by people, dogs, chairs, islands and oceans – many philosophers have doubted whether this picture applies uniformly across all domains. For example, philosophers have questioned whether mathematical truths are made true by an independently existing mathematical reality, whether ethical truths are made true by an independently existing ethical reality, and even whether microphysical truths are made true by an independently existing microscopic reality.

For these philosophers, an alternative account of truth is needed – one which is compatible with some domains lacking a reality independent of the words we use to describe them. The verificationist theory of truth offers such an account. Roughly speaking, the verificationist theory of truth asserts that a sentence is true because our best methods are capable of *verifying it*. For example, verificationists

DOI: 10.4324/9781003190103-4

take the microphysical truths to be exactly those microphysical sentences we are capable of verifying experimentally in the lab. In this section, we explain the verificationist theory of truth in more detail.

4.1.1   VERIFICATION CONDITIONS

Suppose an oak tree is growing in the garden. Someone says 'The tree has nineteen thousand leaves'. There is consensus among speakers about how to verify this statement. Namely, *count the leaves*. If the count ends at 19,000, all competent speakers will accept 'The tree has nineteen thousand leaves' is true.

As another example, consider the statement 'The temperature of the coffee is two hundred degrees'. Again, there is consensus among speakers about how to verify this statement. Namely, *place a thermometer in the coffee*. If the thermometer indicates 200, all competent speakers will accept 'The temperature of the coffee is two hundred degrees' is true.

As a final example, consider the statement 'It is raining'. Once again, there is consensus among speakers about how to verify this statement. Namely, *go outside and look*. If water droplets can be observed falling from the sky, then all competent speakers will accept 'It is raining' is true.

These examples are suggestive of the following general principle:

(Verification Conditions)   For every meaningful sentence, there is a procedure and an outcome such that if the procedure is followed and the outcome is obtained then the community of speakers will agree to accept the sentence.

We refer to the condition that following a sentence's associated procedure would result in its associated outcome as the *verification condition* of the sentence, since it is the condition under which the sentence is considered to be verifiable by the community. Consequently, this general principle is more concisely expressed as the thesis that every meaningful sentence has a verification condition.

⋆ ⋆ *Parenthetical note: Multiple verification conditions.* It is consistent with the thesis that every meaningful sentence has a verification condition that a meaningful sentence has *multiple* verification conditions – which would happen when the community accepts multiple different ways of verifying a sentence. It is likely that in actual fact many sentences have multiple verification conditions. However, for simplicity, we will talk as if a sentence has exactly one verification condition. Everything we say in this chapter easily generalizes to the case of multiple verification conditions. *End note.* ⋆ ⋆

Returning to the previous examples, the verification condition of 'The tree has nineteen thousand leaves' is the condition that following the procedure of counting the leaves would result in the outcome of ending the count at 19,000. The verification condition of 'The temperature of the coffee is two hundred degrees' is the condition that following the procedure of placing a thermometer in the coffee would result in the outcome of the thermometer indicating 200. The verification condition of 'It is raining' is the condition that following the procedure of going outside and looking would result in the observation of water droplets falling from the sky.

4.1.1.1 Soundness

The verification condition of 'p' is *sound* when the verification condition of 'p' obtains only if p. For example, since counting the leaves on a tree accurately determines the number of leaves, the verification condition of 'The tree has nineteen thousand leaves' obtains only if the tree in fact has nineteen thousand leaves. Consequently, the verification condition of 'The tree has nineteen thousand leaves' is sound.

The first point to clarify about verification conditions is that it is not part of the definition of a verification condition that it is sound. Rather, all that is required for a sentence to have a verification condition is that there is some procedure and outcome such that if following the procedure were to result in the outcome, the community of speakers would thereby *accept* the sentence. Thus, it is at least conceivable that the standard for judging the truth of a sentence adopted by the community is *un*sound. For example, it is conceivable that the verification condition of 'The tree has nineteen thousand leaves', perhaps for a tree with special spiritual significance, could have instead been the condition that counting the days since the last solar eclipse results in 19,000 – which clearly gives no reliable indication as to the number of leaves.

4.1.1.2 Measurement and Observation

The second point to clarify about verification conditions is that the procedure associated with a meaningful sentence is not required to be a physical measurement or observation of some kind, such as placing a thermometer in coffee or looking at the sky. Consider, for example, mathematical statements, such as 'There are infinitely many prime numbers'. Mathematical statements entirely concern the properties of *numbers*, which are abstract entities not located in space. Consequently, we do not verify mathematical statements by taking measurements or making observations. Instead, we typically verify mathematical statements by *proving them*.

A full discussion of what mathematical proof involves would take us beyond the scope of this book. But, in brief, a mathematical proof is a sequence of mathematical statements such that each statement in the sequence is either a basic mathematical principle, which all users of mathematical language agree to be true, or else follows logically from earlier statements in the sequence. Thus, we accept a mathematical statement as true when it can be derived by a series of logical deductions from some universally accepted mathematical principles.

As another example, consider aesthetic statements, such as 'The Grand Canyon is beautiful'. In contrast to mathematical statements, it is more controversial what the verification condition of an aesthetic statement would be. One plausible view is that the statement '*x* is beautiful' is accepted as true when the observable properties of *x* satisfy the socially established criteria for beauty. If this is right, then the procedure for verifying '*x* is beautiful' has both an observational and non-observational component. The observational component requires observing *x* to learn its observable properties – primarily, its shape and color. The non-observational component requires evaluating the observable properties of x using the criteria for beauty currently accepted by the community.

4.1.2   TRUTH AS VERIFIABILITY

The verificationist theory of truth presupposes the thesis that every meaningful sentence has a verification condition. This thesis is consistent – at least in principle – with the correspondence and semantic theories of truth. Consider, for example, the sentence 'The temperature of the coffee is two hundred degrees'. Even a correspondence theorist would agree this sentence has a verification condition – namely, the condition that placing a thermometer in the coffee would result in the thermometer indicating 200. Furthermore, since thermometers accurately measure temperature, even a correspondence theorist would agree this verification condition is sound.

Unlike the correspondence and semantic theories of truth, however, the verificationist theory of truth asserts that truth *just is* verifiability. More precisely:

(Verificationist Theory) x is true $=_{df}$ the verification condition of x obtains.[14]

In particular, according to the verificationist theory, 'The tree has nineteen thousand leaves' is true *because* counting the leaves would end at 19,000, 'The temperature of the coffee is two hundred degrees' is true *because* placing a thermometer in the coffee would result in the thermometer indicating 200, 'It is raining' is true *because* going outside and looking would result in the observation of water droplets falling from the sky.

Note that the verificationist theory does not require that every truth has actually been verified. For example, it may so happen that nobody ever goes outside and counts the leaves on the tree. Nevertheless, so long as 19,000 is the number which *would* be obtained, were the count to be performed, the sentence 'The tree has nineteen thousand leaves' remains true.

Although it is not part of the definition of a verification condition that it is sound, the thesis that truth is verifiability entails that every verification condition is in fact sound. This is because, by the T-schema, 'p' is true only if p. Thus, if truth *just is* verifiability then the verification condition of 'p' obtains only if p. Consequently, the verificationist theory of truth collapses the distinction between the way the world really is and the way our best methods take the world to be.

4.2 MOTIVATION

The correspondence and semantic theories both take truth to be responsive, which means that a true sentence 'p' is true because p. In many cases, this is what we would expect. For example, ordinarily we would assume the sentence 'It is raining in London', if true, is true *because* rain is falling in London.

In other cases, however, responsiveness seems more suspect. Consider, for example, the class of aesthetic truths, such as 'The Grand Canyon is beautiful'. It is not obvious that the beauty of the Grand Canyon is an objective feature, akin to its various geological features, which is out there in the world for us to discover. On the contrary, many philosophers believe beauty to be *projected onto* the Grand Canyon by humans.

Something like the following account of how this projection process works is plausible.[15] Whereas predicates such as 'is acidic', 'is liquid' and 'is metallic' are used to label objective features of objects, which existed prior to the invention of language, the predicate 'is beautiful' does not function in this way. Instead, 'is beautiful' is applied to objects which the community of speakers agree should be valued in a certain way. Once speakers reach a consensus on the criteria for determining which objects 'is beautiful' applies to, the sentence 'x is beautiful', for an object x which satisfies these criteria, thereby becomes true. Furthermore, only once 'x is beautiful' becomes true in this manner does the condition that x is beautiful obtain. Thus, in this case, the explanatory direction of the T-schema is reversed: the Grand Canyon is beautiful *because* the sentence 'The Grand Canyon is beautiful' is true, and not the other way around.

We refer to the view that truth constructs domain D as *anti-realism about D*. The previous paragraph discusses anti-realism about aesthetics. But aesthetics is not the only domain towards which philosophers have harbored anti-realist sympathies. Other common targets of anti-realism include ethics, mathematics and quantum physics. The extreme limit of anti-realism is *global anti-realism*, according to which truth constructs *all* domains. For the global anti-realist, even domains as seemingly objective as the macrophysical domain of ordinary objects (tables, chairs, houses, cars, and the like) depend on language for their existence.

Unlike the correspondence and semantic theories, the verificationist theory of truth is compatible with anti-realism about a given domain. Consider, for example, the class of mathematical truths, such as '13 is a factor of 156'. According to the correspondence and semantic theories, this sentence is true because '13' and '156' refer to certain mathematical objects, and these objects independently stand in the relation referred to by 'is a factor of'. Thus, according to the correspondence and semantic theories, '13 is a factor of 156' is true in virtue of an independently existing mathematical reality.

Anti-realists about mathematics doubt the existence of an independently existing mathematical reality – a reality populated by mathematical objects such as the number 13 and the number 156. One reason why mathematical anti-realists doubt the existence of an independent mathematical reality is that it is hard to see how we could possibly know anything about it. After all, numbers are not the kind of thing we bump into on the street. Thus, if numbers exist at all, they exist abstractly, outside of physical space – and it is hard to see how we could form any kind of reliable beliefs about things which make no causal imprint on the physical world.[16]

In contrast to the correspondence and semantic theories, the verificationist theory of truth asserts that '13 is a factor of 156' is true not in virtue of the state of mathematical reality, but rather in virtue of being *verifiable*, which in this case amounts to the fact that following the long division algorithm to divide 156 by 13 and would result in remainder 0. This explanation of the truth of '13 is a factor of 156' makes no reference to an independently existing mathematical reality. Indeed, following the long division algorithm to divide 156 by

13 – a process which can be carried out with pen and paper – would result in remainder 0 even if no independent mathematical reality exists at all. Thus, in contrast to the correspondence and semantic theories, an anti-realist about mathematics could accept the verificationist theory as an account of mathematical truth, maintaining that 13 is a factor of 156 *because* '13 is a factor of 156' is true, which amounts to '13 is a factor of 156' being verifiable.

4.2.1 THE T-SCHEMA

One of the basic desiderata for an analysis of truth is that it has *explanatory power*, in the sense that it reduces the central features of truth to more fundamental, independently plausible, principles. The most central feature of truth is that it satisfies the T-schema

'*p*' is true if and only if *p*.

Consequently, it is a basic desideratum for an analysis of truth as Φ that the Φ-schema

'*p*' is Φ if and only if *p*

follows from independently plausible principles about Φ.

We have already seen that the correspondence and semantic theories satisfy this desideratum, at least for certain fragments of English. In order for the verificationist theory of truth to also satisfy this desideratum, the 'V-schema'

'*p*' is verifiable if and only if *p*

should follow from independently plausible principles regarding verifiability. But does it?

For certain domains, the V-schema *does* have independent plausibility. These are the domains which strike us, for independent reasons, as socially constructed. Consider, for example, the aesthetic domain. As discussed in the previous section, many philosophers consider aesthetic properties, such as *beauty*, to be projected onto reality by humans. This process of projection is plausibly analyzed as follows. There is an agreed upon criterion for classifying an object

x as beautiful – a verification condition for 'x is beautiful' – and the very fact that, for instance, the Grand Canyon satisfies this criterion – the very fact that the verification of 'The Grand Canyon is beautiful' obtains – is what grounds the fact that the Grand Canyon is beautiful. Thus, it is independently plausible that the circumstances under which an object x is beautiful are exactly those circumstances under which 'x is beautiful' is verifiable. Consequently, the verificationist theory of truth explains the T-schema for aesthetic sentences.

The mathematical domain is another case where the V-schema has independent plausibility. As discussed in the previous section, many philosophers doubt mathematical reality exists independently of our methods for determining the truth of mathematical statements. For these philosophers, we develop systems for determining whether mathematical statements are true or false – thereby associating verification conditions with mathematical statements – and it is these systems which are the ultimate source of mathematical reality. For example, on this view, the fact that following the long division algorithm to divide 156 by 13 would result in remainder 0 – i.e., the fact that the verification condition of '13 is a factor of 156' obtains – is what grounds the fact that 13 is a factor of 156. Thus, the V-schema has independent plausibility for mathematical sentences – and consequently the verificationist theory of truth explains the T-schema for mathematical sentences.

However, unlike the aesthetic and mathematical domains, there are domains which do *not* have the strong appearance of being socially constructed. Consider, for example, the astrophysical domain of stars, planets, comets, and so on. The vast majority of philosophers consider the astrophysical domain to exist independently of the methods humans use to form beliefs about it. Consider, for example, the fact that the Sun is composed of plasma. Almost no-one thinks that *this* fact depends in any way on the scientific instruments and theories humans have developed to form beliefs about the Sun. The Sun would still be made of plasma even if tomorrow we decided to burn all our physics textbooks and return to a primitive view of the Sun as a supernatural entity.

Consequently, the astrophysical domain is one example of a domain for which there could *prima facie* be a gap between the reality of that domain and the way our best methods take that domain to be. Other examples include the biological domain and the domain of everyday macroscopic objects – chairs, tables, cars, and the like. For sentences in these domains, there is no obvious guarantee that the V-schema holds in general. As a result, the verificationist theory of truth does not seem to offer an explanation of the T-schema for these domains.

4.3   ARGUMENT FOR THE VERIFIABILITY ANSWER

The central argument for the verificationist theory of truth is the *manifestation argument*, originally due to Michael Dummett, the most prominent proponent of the verificationist theory in the second half of the Twentieth Century:

(1)   Understanding a sentence consists in knowing its verification condition.
(2)   If understanding a sentence consists in knowing its verification condition then the meaning of a sentence *just is* its verification condition.
(3)   The meaning of a sentence is its verification condition. [From (1), (2)]
(4)   The truth of a sentence depends on its meaning.
(5)   The truth of a sentence depends on its verification condition. [From (3), (4)]
(6)   If the truth of a sentence depends on its verification condition then truth is verifiability.

---

(7)   Truth is verifiability. [From (5), (6)]

4.3.1   REASONS FOR BELIEVING THE PREMISES

4.3.1.1 Premise (1)

According to premise (1), to understand a sentence is to know how it can in principle be verified. For example, to understand 'The tree has nineteen thousand leaves' is to know that if counting the leaves on the tree were to result in 19,000 then the sentence would be accepted by the community.

Premise (1) is motivated by the observation that, at least in some cases, we plausibly learn the meaning of an expression by – in effect – learning how to verify sentences containing that expression. For example, it is plausible that we learn the meaning of quantificational expressions like 'there are five', 'there are seven' and 'there are fifty' by learning how to count. Similarly, it is plausible that we learn the meaning of 'It is raining' by – in effect – learning that it is verified by going outside and having the kinds of perceptual experiences associated with water droplets falling from the sky.

4.3.1.2 Premise (2)

We can argue for premise (2) as follows. Suppose understanding a sentence consists in knowing its verification condition. Since to understand a sentence is to know its meaning, it follows that knowing the meaning of a sentence consists in knowing its verification condition. It seems to follow immediately that the meaning of a sentence *just is* its verification condition.

4.3.1.3 Premise (4)

Premise (4) fits into our common sense conception of truth. For example, ordinarily we would expect that changing the meaning of 'Venice is sinking' could result in it having a different truth-status, even if the reality of Venice remains unchanged. In particular, if we changed the meaning of 'sinking' so that it instead meant *rising*, then 'Venice is sinking' would instead mean that *Venice is rising* – and so no longer be true.

4.3.1.4 Premise (5)

We can argue for premise (5) as an inference to the best explanation. Suppose the truth of a sentence depends on its verification condition. Then whether a sentence is true depends on how we would go about verifying it. In particular, whether 'The temperature of the coffee is 200 degrees' is true depends on how we decide to measure temperature. The simplest and most plausible explanation for this seems to be that truth *just is* verifiability.

4.4 EVALUATION

In this section, we evaluate both the manifestation argument for the verifiability answer and the verifiability answer itself.

4.4.1 EVALUATION OF THE ARGUMENT

Since premises (2), (4) and (6) are all highly plausible, the weight of the manifestation argument rests on premise (1). To refute premise (1), it suffices to find an example of a sentence whose meaning we understand despite the fact the sentence lacks an agreed-upon procedure for verifying it. In fact, many sentences which describe philosophical views seem to fall into this category. Consider, for example, the sentence 'Non-physical minds exist'. Although this sentence is surely meaningful, there does not appear to be any way to verify it. Certainly, a non-physical mind could not be detected by any scientific instrument. Furthermore, unlike the case of mathematical statements, we do not have some agreed-upon procedure for proving whether or not there are non-physical minds.

4.4.1.1 A Possible Reply

A possible reply on behalf of the verificationist – one that many early verificationists enthusiastically adopted – is to simply reject the assumption that the sentence 'Non-physical minds exist' is meaningful. According to this view, although 'Non-physical minds exist' appears meaningful to us, this is really a kind of illusion. Likewise, 'Humans have free will', 'God exists', 'Time flows in one direction', and so on, are all condemned to the realm of the meaningless, since there is no agreement on what would constitute conclusive evidence of their truth.

One problem with this reply is that it is in tension with the principle that the meaning of a sentence is determined by the meanings of the words in the sentence and the way those words are arranged. This principle is referred to as *compositionality*. Consider, for example, the sentence 'Non-physical minds exist'. Plausibly, 'physical', 'mind' and 'exist' are are all meaningful words. Consequently, 'non-physical' should also be meaningful, since applying 'non-' to 'physical' simply inverts the meaning of 'physical' to its opposite.

But then 'Non-physical minds exist' is meaningful after all, since it combines meaningful words in a grammatical way.

The motivation for compositionality is that it explains why speakers are able to understand sentences they have never seen before. Consider, for example, the following sentence:

> There are thirteen blue dogs in Paris.

Most likely, this is the first time you have ever seen this sentence. Nevertheless, you immediately knew what it meant. The only viable explanation for this appears to be compositionality: you already knew the meanings of 'there are', 'thirteen', 'blue', 'dog', 'in', 'Paris', and combined these meanings together in a systematic way to obtain the meaning of 'There are thirteen blue dogs in Paris'.

4.4.2   EVALUATION OF THE ANSWER

We now discuss two objections to the verificationist theory of truth, which apply regardless of the argument used in support of it.

4.4.2.1 Undecidable Statements

Ordinarily we would assume one of the following sentences is true:

(H)   Henry VIII sneezed at 2:11pm on 03/05/1537

(¬H)   It is not the case that Henry VIII sneezed at 2:11pm on 03/05/1537.

Consequently, by the verificationist theory of truth, either (H) is verifiable or (¬H) is verifiable. These statements would be verified by trustworthy historical records detailing Henry VIII's daily behaviors. Thus, the verificationist theory entails that either there exists a trustworthy historical record of Henry VIII sneezing at 2:11pm on 03/05/1537 or there exists a trustworthy historical record of Henry VIII *not* sneezing at 2:11pm on 03/05/1537. Clearly, however, it is almost certain that no such records exist. Consequently, it is almost certain that the verificationist theory is false.

This, in a nutshell, is the objection to the verificationist theory of truth from undecidable statements – an undecidable statement being a statement, like (H), such that neither it nor its negation is verifiable.

4.4.2.1.1 A Possible Reply   The only response available to the verificationist is to reject the assumption that either (H) or (¬H) is true. Equivalently, given the T-schema, the verificationist must reject the assumption that the following sentence is true:

(H∨¬H)   Either Henry VIII sneezed at 2:11pm on 03/05/1537 or it is not the case that Henry VIII sneezed at 2:11pm on 03/05/1537.

It may come as a surprise to you that verificationists reject (H∨¬H), since (H ∨¬H) is typically considered a truth of logic. More generally, it is typically assumed to be a basic law of logic that for any sentence '*p*', the sentence '*p* or not *p*' is true. This law is known as the *law of excluded middle*.

The law of excluded middle is plausible because, ordinarily, we think of reality as completely filled in, with every question decided. For example, ordinarily we suppose that either the tree has nineteen thousand leaves or it does not, either the coffee is two hundred degrees or it is not, either it is raining or it is not. Verificationists must therefore reject the assumption that reality is completely filled in. In particular, since the available evidence does not settle the question of whether Henry VIII sneezed at 2:11pm on 03/05/1537, verificationists must accept there is no fact of the matter as to whether Henry VIII sneezed at 2:11pm on 03/05/1537: the relevant reality is simply *absent*.

This consequence of the verificationist theory of truth can be explained by *anti-realism about the past*. According to this view, if '*p*' is a statement about the past then whether *p* is determined by whether '*p*' is true, which in turn is determined by whether '*p*' is verifiable. In particular, JFK was assassinated on November 22nd 1963 *because* there is photographic evidence of the event occurring, Henry VIII had six wives *because* reliable historical records indicate these marriages took place and dinosaurs existed 100 million years ago *because* dinosaur fossils date to this period. Thus, rather than having an independent existence, the past is generated by the presently existing historical evidence. This explains why missing historical evidence correlates with gaps in the past.[17]

4.4.2.2 Fitch's Paradox

Since counting the leaves on the tree would deliver some definite number, there is some number n such that the sentence 'The tree has n leaves' is true. Furthermore, this is the case even for a tree whose leaves have never actually been counted. So the verificationist theory of truth is committed to the existence of truths which have never actually been verified.

This consequence of the verificationist theory of truth leads to a paradox, known as *Fitch's paradox*. Consider a truth which has not been verified, such as 'The tree has nineteen thousand leaves'. Then the following sentence is true:

(F) The tree has nineteen thousand leaves and 'The tree has nineteen thousand leaves' has not been verified.

So, by the verificationist theory, (F) is verifiable. Thus, there is a possible future in which (F) has been verified – a possible future in which the verification procedure of (F) is actually performed. But verifying (F) automatically verifies both conjuncts of (F). So there is a possible future in which both of the following sentences have been verified:

(F1) The tree has nineteen thousand leaves.

(F2) 'The tree has nineteen thousand leaves' has not been verified.

But if (F2) has been verified then it is verifiable and so, by the verificationist theory, is true. Therefore (F2) is true in this possible future – and so, by the T-schema, in this future 'The tree has nineteen thousand leaves' has not been verified. Consequently, in this possible future 'The tree has nineteen thousand leaves' both has and has not been verified, which is impossible.

4.4.2.2.1 A Possible Reply   An essential component of Fitch's paradox is the inference from

(F) The tree has nineteen thousand leaves and 'The tree has nineteen thousand leaves' has not been verified.

to

(T) The sentence (F) is true.

This inference is justified by the T-schema. However, recall from Section 1.3.8 that, due to the liar paradox, the T-schema runs into trouble when applied to sentences which themselves contain truth-related vocabulary. According to the verificationist theory of truth, 'has not been verified' is truth-related vocabulary. Thus, there is no guarantee that the above inference is in fact legitimate. Whether it is legitimate depends on how verificationists decide to solve the liar paradox. It might therefore turn out that verificationists can resolve the liar paradox in such a way that Fitch's paradox is also blocked.

4.5   CHAPTER SUMMARY

In this chapter, we introduced the verificationist theory of truth, according to which truth consists in verifiability. We clarified the nature of verifiability and observed that, unlike the correspondence and semantic theories, the verificationist theory of truth is compatible with anti-realism about a given domain – in the sense that truth constructs rather than merely responds to that domain. We then outlined Dummett's manifestation argument for the verificationist theory of truth and discussed some objections to the argument. Finally, we outlined some objections to the verificationist theory of truth more generally – in particular, the objection from undecidable statements and the objection from Fitch's paradox.

NOTES

14. More generally, when it is allowed that a sentence can have multiple verification conditions:

$$x \text{ is true } =_{df} \text{ one of the verification conditions of } x \text{ obtains.}$$

15. This account of projection is due to Douglas Edwards, *The Metaphysics of Truth* (Oxford University Press: Oxford, 2018).

16. See Section 2.4.2 for a longer discussion of this point.

17. For an extended discussion of truths about the past in the context of the verificationist theory of truth, see Michael Dummett, *Truth and the Past*, (Columbia University Press: Columbia, 2005).

FURTHER READING

- Historical background: Michael Dummett, *Truth and Other Enigmas* (Harvard University Press: Cambridge, MA, 1978).
- Classic work: Crispin Wright, *Truth and Objectivity* (Harvard University Press: Cambridge, MA, 1994); Michael Devitt, *Realism and Truth* (Princeton University Press: Princeton, NJ, 1996); Timothy Williamson, 'Intuitionism Disproved?' *Analysis*, Vol. 42, No. 4, pp. 203–207, 1982.
- Contemporary discussion: Douglas Edwards, *The Metaphysics of Truth* (Oxford University Press: Oxford, 2018).

TRANSPARENCY

5.1 ANSWER TO THE CENTRAL QUESTION

The correspondence, semantic, and verificationist theories of truth are all *substantive* theories of truth, in the sense that they provide an answer to the central question: a feature shared by all and only the truths, which makes them true. By contrast, the transparency theory of truth rejects the underlying assumption that there *is* a feature shared by all and only the truths, which makes them true. Instead, the transparency theory takes truth to be 'transparent', in the sense that for it to be the case that '*p*' is true *just is* for it to be the case that *p*: for 'Snow is white' to be true *just is* for snow to be white, for 'Inflation is rising' to be true *just is* for inflation to be rising, for 'Sugar is soluble' to be true *just is* for sugar to be soluble, and so on.

5.2 MOTIVATION

The transparency account of truth is motivated by the thought that, were it not for the finite limitations of human inquiry, the 'true'-free fragment of our language is perfectly sufficient for describing reality completely. One way of putting the point is that God, being completely unfettered by limitations of time or memory or knowledge,

DOI: 10.4324/9781003190103-5

could describe all of reality in full without ever *using* the truth predicate. Of course, given that our language in fact has a truth predicate, God would *mention* the truth predicate; however, God would not need to *use* the truth predicate at all in the full description of reality.

★ ★ *Parenthetical note: Use and mention.* One uses the word 'word' when one mentions it, just as one uses Agnes' name – namely, 'Agnes' – when one mentions Agnes by name. Agnes is a cat; 'Agnes' is a word and not a cat. Along these lines, there are 10 alphabetical letters (counting the space character) in the name 'Notre Dame' but there are no alphabetical letters in the makeup of Notre Dame itself. Likewise, the third letter of 'the third letter of' is exactly the same letter as the fifth letter of 'Notre'. If one mentions the fifth letter of 'Notre' one can do so by the description ' the fifth letter of 'Notre' ' or by using its standard quotation name, which is 'e', which, of course, is spelled ' 'e' '. We leave further examples of *using* versus *mentioning* to the reader. We note only that sometimes one can use and mention a word at the same time, as we do when we hereby mention the last word of this very sentence. *End note.* ★ ★

How can God successfully describe all of reality without using the truth predicate? The question demands reflection. (Readers should pause and so reflect! Really.) One way of seeing the answer, at least from the transparency perspective, is to consider the full description of your house:

- The house has *n* many rooms, the full description of which are as follows (and herein follow the full descriptions of such rooms).
- The house has *n* many exterior walls and roofs, the full description of which are as follows (and herein follow full descriptions).
- The house has *n* many windows, the full description...etc.
- ....etc.

Wherein does the truth predicate show up? It doesn't, or if it does, it does so in an *eliminable* way. What does 'eliminable' mean here? The answer points to what transparency theorists see as the central feature of truth, namely, the so-called transparency rule:

(Transparency Rule)   Let Tr be the truth predicate. Let φ be any sentence and $\ulcorner\varphi\urcorner$ be a name of φ. Then φ and $Tr(\ulcorner\varphi\urcorner)$ are *intersubstitutable* in all (non-opaque) contexts: putting the one for the other results in a sentence with the same content.[18]

To say, as above, that an occurrence of 'true' is *eliminable* is to say that it is *eliminable by applications of the transparency rule*.

Return to the example of God fully describing your house. Suppose that in the full description the following claims are required:

- The walls of Room 2 are painted blue.
- The walls of Room 3 are painted green.
- The walls of Room 4 are painted white.

By the transparency rule, God certainly could've said

- 'The walls of Room 2 are painted blue' is true.
- 'The walls of Room 3 are painted green' is true.
- 'The walls of Room 4 are painted white' is true.

But why? Adding 'is true' is just a *more wordy* way of saying what is said without it. Or so goes the central thought of the transparency theory, according to which truth – that is, whatever is expressed by the transparency-rule-governed predicate 'true' – is not in any way an *explanatory* property; it's just a device that affords alternative ways of saying things that can, at least in principle (and certainly by God), be said without it.

If, as above, God could describe all of reality without using the truth predicate, why do we have the truth predicate in our language? Is it merely stylistic? Is it like a bell that ones ties to something to make it more conspicuous? The answer turns on our de facto finitude. God is beyond limitation. We humans are significantly limited, not just in terms of time constraints (e.g., we only have so much time to describe reality), but also memory, knowledge, and the like. These limitations, according to the transparency theory, explain the utility of the 'truth device' in our language.

Consider an example different from your house, the full description of which is finite (and probably not even a very large finite description). According to one theory of negation (i.e., the 'not' connective) and disjunction (i.e., the 'or' connective), every instance of the following form is true (where φ is any sentence, $\neg$ is negation, and $\vee$ is disjunction):

$$\varphi \vee \neg\varphi$$

Challenge: on the assumption that there are more instances of the above form than you have moments of time in your lifetime, try to express what was just expressed without using the truth predicate, namely, the law of excluded middle:

LEM.   All instances of $\varphi \vee \neg\varphi$ are true.

Result: you failed. But the failure is not your fault. It's practically impossible to meet the challenge. Why? Because the only way you can successfully express what's expressed by LEM but without the truth predicate is to express each and every instance, such as

- Either grass is green or it's not the case that grass is green; and
- either grass is blue or it's not the case that grass is blue; and
- either grass is purple or it's not the case that grass is purple; and
- either grass is orange or it's not the case that grass is orange; and...
- ....

and so on. Of course, God can express LEM without using 'true' by simply zipping off all instances of LEM – and God can do so in lightening quick fashion. But we humans don't have such capacity. And that's the reason – *and on the transparency theory, the essential reason* – that 'true' was introduced into our language. The device lets us express very long (even infinitely long) descriptions of reality in very short fashion.

But it's not just really long descriptions of reality for which 'true' proves its practical utility. The device is useful when you don't know or simply can't remember the full description. For example, you might know that Max said something true yesterday, but you can't remember what it was. The truth device allows you to express as much by simply saying that Max said something true yesterday even though you can't remember what it was. (Try saying that without the truth predicate! Again, were you God, you'd be able to do it.)

In the end, the transparency theory is motivated by the thought that all of reality is completely describable without using the truth predicate; however, the truth predicate – or, more telling, the 'truth device' – is a tool that was introduced via the transparency rule to overcome our finite limitations. The truth predicate does not express a property that *explains* anything; it simply serves to express explanations of things. Truth is not itself an explanation of anything despite being used in many explanations. Were we as unlimited as God, we could do away with 'true' entirely – unless we just wanted to hear the ring of it for some reason.

The upshot of all this for the central question is that, given the transparency theory, *there is no feature* shared by all and only the the truths, which makes them all true. Consider, for example, the sentences 'Water has a higher boiling point than ammonia' and 'Paris is the capital of France'. Given the transparency theory, to assert that the first sentence is true *just is* to assert that water has a higher boiling point than ammonia. Similarly, to assert that the second sentence is true *just is* to assert that Paris is the capital of France. Clearly, there is no common explanation for why water has a higher boiling point than ammonia and Paris is the capital of France – the former is explained by the chemical constitution of the two substances and the second is explained by the decisions of the French government. Thus, there is no common explanation for why 'Water has a higher boiling point that ammonia' and 'Paris is the capital of France' are both true.

5.3   ARGUMENT FOR THE TRANSPARENCY ANSWER

There are various arguments for the transparency theory, some of which rest on alleged failures of alternative theories of truth (e.g., correspondence, semantic, verificationist). We point to just one argument (due especially to contemporary philosopher Hartry Field).

The argument is Ockham-ish: it's a good methodological practice to assume that truth is no more than what's given by the simple transparency rule *unless* there's good reason to do otherwise. In premise–conclusion form:

(1) The transparency theory is the simplest theory of truth which explains the phenomena associated with truth.

(2) For any feature F, we ought to accept the simplest theory of F which explains the phenomena associated with F.

---

(3) We ought to accept the transparency theory of truth. [From (1), (2)]

Note that the conclusion of the argument is not that the transparency theory is *true*, but rather that we ought to accept the transparency theory. This distinguishes the argument for the transparency theory from other arguments seen in this book so far.

5.3.1 REASONS FOR BELIEVING THE PREMISES

5.3.1.1 Premise (1)

What are the phenomena associated with truth? At a minimum, any theory of truth should explain why the instances of the T-schema hold:

'p' is true if and only if p.

The transparency theory provides a satisfying explanation for the T-schema. It is a basic law of logic that any condition is materially equivalent to itself:

p if and only if p.

But, according to the transparency theory, φ and $Tr(\ulcorner \varphi \urcorner)$ have exactly the same content, and so one can always be substituted for the other.[19] In particular, replacing the condition that p in the above logical law with the condition that 'p' is true leaves us with an equivalent sentence:

'p' is true if and only if p.

But this is just the T-schema!

5.3.1.2 Premise (2)

Premise (2) can be supported by typical Ockham-like examples. Suppose you're in a theatre and the play has just ended, the cast has just bowed, and the curtains close in front of them. In the next moment, the curtains, while remaining closed, are moving in a ruffling way, and shuffling-feet noises are coming from behind the curtain. One explanation: the behavior of the cast behind the curtain is making both the ruffling-curtain effect and the feet-shuffling noises. Another explanation: the cast are making the curtain move and the feet-shuffling noises, but they are doing that because a silent elephant has entered the stage behind the curtain and is pushing them. An Ockham-Razor argument pushes for the first, simpler explanation over the otherwise unmotivated one. Should recalcitrant data demand the more involved account then so be it. But until then, stick with the simpler one.

5.4   EVALUATION

There are at least two central lines to evaluate: the argument for the transparency theory, and the transparency theory itself. In this section, we evaluate both.

5.4.1   EVALUATION OF THE ARGUMENT

Since premise (2) of the argument is highly plausible, we focus on critiquing premise (1). An objection to premise (1) would either be an example of an explanatorily adequate theory of truth which is simpler than the transparency theory *or* an example of a truth-related phenomenon which is not explained by the transparency theory. It is hard to see how any theory of truth could be simpler than the transparency theory. Thus, the only viable objection to (1) is an example of a truth-related phenomenon which falls outside the scope of the transparency theory. We discuss one purported example of such a phenomenon: the fact that truth is *valuable*.

5.4.1.1 The Value of Truth

The common sense view that truth is valuable can be made precise in various ways. We'll discuss two: 'truth as the aim of inquiry' and the 'pragmatic/instrumental value of truth'. Each in turn.

5.4.1.1.1 Truth as the Aim of Inquiry   Rational inquiry is truth-directed in the sense that we seek only *true* descriptions of reality. In a slogan: the aim of rational inquiry is truth. In this way, there is 'value' in truth: it's the 'normative end' of rational inquiry.

The objection to the transparency account is that it cannot accommodate the value of truth so understood. After all, if the transparency account were to acknowledge the value of truth – as the aim of rational inquiry – then the account would thereby acknowledge that there is something importantly *explanatory* about truth. Specifically, if truth is the end of rational inquiry then the property of truth partly explains rational inquiry; truth is an essential ingredient in the full explanation of what makes for rational inquiry. But the transparency theory maintains that there's no explanatory work done by truth; the only work it does is exhausted by its role in allowing limited beings like us to express otherwise practically inexpressible descriptions of reality. (Recall the expression of LEM or the like.)

5.4.1.1.2 Truth as Instrumentally Valuable   Another way in which the 'value of truth' can be understood is instrumentally. In particular, agents with true beliefs navigate about the world more efficiently than those with untrue beliefs. A value of truth is therefore instrumental; truth explains what it is about the beliefs of efficient navigators that makes them efficient.

The objection to the transparency account is that it cannot accommodate the given instrumental value of truth so understood. As with rational inquiry, if truth explains the difference between the beliefs of efficient worldly navigators from less efficient ones then truth is explanatory, contrary to the transparency theory.

5.4.1.1.3 A Possible Reply   A possible reply to both of the value-of-truth objections pushes for details of the principles being invoked in the objections. Consider, for example, the end-of-inquiry slogan:

E1.   Truth is the aim of rational inquiry.

E1 is certainly true. The question concerns the *role* of 'truth' in E1. A transparency theorist is likely to note that 'truth' in E1 is in fact just playing its usual expressive role, even if the surface grammar of E1 might hide the role a bit. In particular, a transparency theorist is likely to claim that E1 is simply shorthand for the following equivalent principle:

E2. Rational inquiry aims to achieve a theory which only contains true sentences.

What role is 'true' playing in E2? The answer is exactly as transparency theorists say: namely, its expressive role. In particular, E2 is short-hand for the following infinitely long sentence:

E3. Rational inquiry aims to achieve a theory which contains 'Grass is green' only if grass is green, contains 'Grass is blue' only if grass is blue, contains 'Grass is yellow' only if grass is yellow,...etc.

The equivalence between E2 and E3 is underpinned by the transparency rule. Applying the transparency rule to E3, we obtain:

E4. Rational inquiry aims to achieve a theory which contains 'Grass is green' only if 'Grass is green' is true, contains 'Grass is blue' only if 'Grass is blue' is true, contains 'Grass is yellow' only if 'Grass is yellow' is true,...etc.

E4 in turn is equivalent to

E5. Rational inquiry aims to achieve a theory such that for any sentence φ, the theory contains φ only if φ is true.

which is just a re-phrasing of E3.

Again, *we*, in our limited situation, use the truth predicate because we can't otherwise express the infinitely long E3. But God can, thereby refuting the idea that 'true' is somehow essential or otherwise importantly explanatory.

The same reply applies to the instrumental-value objection. In that case, the transparency theorist notes that the role of 'true' in the target principle

B1. For any sentence φ, if φ is true then, all else equal, believing φ makes one a more efficient navigator of the world than not believing φ.

is just its usual expressive role. In particular, 'true' in B1 is doing a similar sort of abbreviating work to 'true' in E2, in this case abbreviating the infinitely long

B2. If grass is green then, all else equal, believing 'Grass is green' makes one a more efficient navigator of the world than not believing 'Grass is green'; and if Grass is blue then, all else equal, believing 'Grass is blue' makes one a more efficient navigator of the world than not believing 'Grass is blue'; and if grass is yellow then, all else equal, believing 'Grass is yellow' makes one a more efficient navigator of the world than not believing 'Grass is yellow'; and...so on.

Applying the transparency rule to B2, we obtain

B3. If 'Grass is green' is true then, all else equal, believing 'Grass is green' makes one a more efficient navigator of the world than not believing 'Grass is green'; and if 'Grass is blue' is true then, all else equal, believing 'Grass is blue' makes one a more efficient navigator of the world than not believing 'Grass is blue'; and if 'Grass is yellow' is true then, all else equal, believing 'Grass is yellow' makes one a more efficient navigator of the world than not believing 'Grass is yellow'; and...so on.

which is straightforwardly equivalent to B1.

In the end, the transparency theorist will likely reply to both value-of-truth objections by showing how to eliminate the use of 'true' by way of the transparency rule. And if 'true' really is eliminable (so that God could say the same thing without using 'true') then 'true' is not expressing any explanatory property in such 'value principles', but rather just helping to express such principles.

5.4.2 EVALUATION OF THE ANSWER

The objection from the value of truth, by attempting to present a truth-related phenomenon which is incompatible with the transparency theory, doubles as an objection *both* to premise (1) of the argument for the transparency theory *and* to the transparency theory itself. In this section we discuss three more objections to the transparency theory, which apply regardless of the argument given in support of it.

5.4.2.1 Peculiarity

The first objection to the transparency account is that it makes truth spectacularly peculiar. After all, except for 'true' all predicates in our language are explanatory in the sense that they are essentially involved in some explanation of some part of reality. Not all explanations are interesting or important, but they're still explanatory. Consider any predicate other than 'true'. Take the predicate 'is sitting'. This is not generally thought to be an important explanatory predicate; however, it certainly expresses a property that figures in some explanations of reality. Example: why does Max have such-n-so shape against such-n-such chair? Answer: Max is sitting. This might not be a deep or significant or 'fundamental' explanation of Max's shape vis-a-vis the chair; however, it's an explanation. And one could find such 'explanatory power' in any predicate *except*, if the transparency account is correct, for 'true'. But that's just making for an unexplained deviation in the way predicates work in our language.

5.4.2.1.1 A Possible Reply   The objection challenges the transparency theorist to come up with some explanation of the remarkable abnormality of 'true' as compared with all other predicates in the language. (Note that the challenge goes through even if *most* predicates are explanatory to some degree. We've just simplified to *all other predicates* for convenience.) The challenge is fair and important.

A possible reply is that 'true' expresses a 'logical property' in the sense that the predicate is abstracted from logical vocabulary, and in particular from logic's (logically redundant) *it is true that* connective. Just as nobody reasonably expects conjunction ('and') or disjunction ('or') to be explanatory in any fashion, so too for any predicate that is 'abstracted from' such connectives.

How does one 'abstract' the truth predicate from the *it is true that* connective? The idea is that one tries to have the predicate behave as close to the connective as possible (i.e., as grammatically possible). Just as the truth connective is logically redundant, in the sense that, when † symbolizes 'it is true that', $\dagger\varphi$ is logically equivalent to φ, one tries to mirror such redundancy in the truth predicate, and one obvious way of doing so is via the transparency rule: just as $\dagger\varphi$ and φ are *logically equivalent*, so too $Tr(\ulcorner\varphi\urcorner)$ and φ are intersubstitutable according to the extended entailment relation governing the new truth predicate Tr.

The transparency theorist replies to the given challenge by pointing out the source of the truth predicate. Since nobody reasonably expects logical vocabulary to be explanatory – and instead expects such vocabulary just to 'allow for expression of explanations' (by connecting up other genuinely explanatory parts of the language) – one should likewise not expect predicates that are built to do nothing more than mimic such logical vocabulary to be explanatory.

5.4.2.2 Meaning Sensitivity

According to the transparency theory, φ and $Tr(\ulcorner\varphi\urcorner)$ are everywhere intersubstitutable. In particular, since every condition is necessarily equivalent to itself –

> Necessarily, p if and only if p

– the transparency theory entails that the truth of 'p' is true is necessarily equivalent to the condition that p:

> Necessarily, 'p' is true if and only if p.

This runs counter to the common sense view, previously referred to as *meaning sensitivity*, that whether 'p' is true depends in some way on the *meaning* of 'p' – i.e., holding fixed the state of the world but varying the meaning of 'p' is one way to vary the truth status of 'p'.[20] Consider, for example, the sentence 'Seawater is salty'. According to meaning sensitivity, if we changed the meaning of 'salty' to *sweet* then 'Seawater is salty' would no longer be true – even though the salt-content of seawater remains unchanged. By contrast, according to the transparency theory, if we changed the meaning of 'salty' to *sweet* then, since the saltiness of seawater would be unaffected by this linguistic decision, seawater would remain salty, and so 'Seawater is salty' would remain true.

5.4.2.2.1 A Possible Reply   The meaning sensitivity objection asks us to consider a possible world w which is as close as possible to the actual world, but for the fact that in w 'salty' means *sweet* rather than *salty*. We are then asked to consider whether in w the sentence 'Seawater is salty' is true. Since changing the meaning of 'salty' does not change the salt-content of seawater, everyone accepts:

(1) In w: seawater is salty.

Thus, by the transparency rule, the transparency theorist accepts

(2) In w: 'Seawater is salty' is true.

Furthermore, everyone also accepts

(3) In w: 'Seawater is salty' means 'Seawater is sweet' and seawater is not sweet.

But, in combination with meaning sensitivity, (3) entails

(4) In w: 'Seawater is salty' is not true.

which contradicts (2). Therefore the transparency theory is incompatible with meaning sensitivity.

In response to this objection, a transparency theorist will want to carefully distinguish the question of whether 'Seawater is salty' is true from the question of whether 'Seawater is salty' *means something true*. Although these questions seem the same, a transparency theorist will in fact answer them differently. Since seawater is salty in w, a transparency theorist accepts that 'Seawater is salty' is true in w. By contrast, since 'Seawater is salty' means in w that *seawater is sweet*, a transparency theorist will not accept that 'Seawater is salty' means something true in w.

To see this, note that, by the transparency rule, (3) entails

(5) In w: 'Seawater is salty' means 'Seawater is sweet' and 'Seawater is sweet' is not true.

which in turn entails

(5)   There exists φ such that in w: 'Seawater is salty' means φ and φ
       is not true.

A transparency theorist can therefore explain why meaning sensitivity
is intuitively correct, despite being false. Ordinarily, we conflate the
question of whether a sentence is true with the question of whether
a sentence means something true. Clearly, changing the meaning
of a sentence can change whether it means something true. Consequently, as a result of the aforementioned conflation, we wrongly
infer that changing the meaning of a sentence can change whether it
itself is true.

5.4.2.3 Responsiveness

According to the responsiveness hypothesis, for any sentence 'p',
whether 'p' is true is determined by whether p. Responsiveness forms
part of our common-sense conception of truth. However, responsiveness is incompatible with the transparency theory. To see why,
consider the sentence 'Snow is white'. By responsiveness,

> 'Snow is white' is true because snow is white.

But, by an application of the transparency rule, this entails

> Snow is white because snow is white

which is false: explanation is *irreflexive*, in the sense that nothing can
explain itself.

5.4.2.3.1 A Possible Reply   Responsiveness is appealing because,
ordinarily, we take questions about truth to more fundamentally
be questions about the non-linguistic world: we are interested in
whether 'God exists' is true because we are interested in whether
God exists, we are interested in whether 'There is extra-terrestrial
life' is true because we are interested in whether *there is extra-terrestrial
life*, and so on. Responsiveness explains why questions of truth
really amount to questions about the world: whether 'p' is true is
determined by whether p.

In response, a transparency theorist will likely point out that
the transparency theory *also* explains why questions of truth really

amount to questions about the world. On the transparency theory, for 'p' to be true *just is* for it to be the case that p. Consequently, the question of whether 'p' is true is *the very same question* as the question of whether p.

5.5 CHAPTER SUMMARY

In this chapter, we introduced the transparency theory of truth, according to which there is no answer to the central question – no feature common to all and only the truths, which makes them true. Instead, for 'p' to be true *just is* for it to be the case that p. Thus, since there is no common explanation for why seawater is salty and increasing interest rates lowers inflation, there is no common explanation for why 'Seawater is salty' and 'Increasing interest rates lowers inflation' are both true.

We outlined an argument for the transparency theory of truth on the basis that it is always best to accept the simplest adequate explanation of a given phenomenon – and the transparency theory is the simplest adequate explanation of truth. We then discussed an objection both to this argument and to the transparency theory more generally – namely, that the transparency theory fails to account for the value of truth (and hence is not an *adequate* explanation of truth). In addition, we discussed three further objections to the transparency theory itself: the objection from peculiarity, the objection from meaning sensitivity and the objection from responsiveness.

NOTES

18. Two points of clarification:
    1. $Tr(x)$ means 'x is true'.
    2. A so-called opaque context is (for present purposes) one in which otherwise valid substitutions break down. A common example involves 'believes that' contexts: Louis Lane believes that Superman flies but she doesn't believe that Clark Kent flies even though Superman is Clark Kent.

19. Subject to the usual qualification that the substitution does not occur inside the scope of an opaque connective like 'Sally believes that'.

20. If meaning sensitivity is elevated to the status of a truth-related phenomenon to be explained by any adequate theory of truth then this objection also works as an objection to premise (1) of the argument for the transparency theory. However, we take the view that meaning sensitivity is too controversial to be considered a neutral phenomenon which any adequate theory of truth ought to explain.

5.6 FURTHER READING

- Historical background: Frank P. Ramsey, 'Facts and Propositions', *Aristotelian Society Supplementary Volume*, Vol. 7, pp. 153–170, 1927; Willard van Orman Quine *Philosophy of Logic* (Prentice Hall: Hoboken, NJ, 1970).
- Classic work: Paul Horwich, *Truth* (Clarendon Press: Oxford, 1998); Stephen Leeds 'Theories of Reference and Truth', *Erkenntnis*, Vol. 13, No. 1, pp. 111–129, 1978.
- Contemporary discussion: Jc Beall, *Spandrels of Truth* (Oxford University Press: Oxford, 2009); Hartry Field, *Saving Truth from Paradox* (Oxford University Press: Oxford, 2008).

PLURALITY

6.1 ANSWER TO THE CENTRAL QUESTION

The central question: what feature, if any, do all and only the truths have in common, which makes them all true? On the *pluralist* theory of truth, there isn't one answer but many.[21] In particular, 'the' true answer to the central question requires the following answers:

- Truth, for some domain of sentences, is *correspondence to the facts.*
- Truth, for some domain of sentences, is *semantic correctness.*
- Truth, for some domain of sentences, is *verifiability.*
- Truth, for some domain of sentences, is *transparent.*

In short, once we fix the domain of sentences under discussion (e.g., sentences concerning macro-physical phenomena and aesthetic-focused sentences) the property common to all and only the truths *in the given domain* is such-n-so; however, there are at least a few different domains that demand different accounts of truth.

6.2 MOTIVATION

A common motivation for pluralism arises from apparent differences between different sorts of properties. For example, aesthetic

DOI: 10.4324/9781003190103-6

properties can sometimes appear to be 'constructed' in ways that, for example, properties of macro-physical objects (e.g., mass and weight) do not appear to be constructed.[22] Similarly, properties like 'is tall' can appear to be different in kind from properties of mathematical objects, such as 'is a natural number less than 5' or the like. And with apparent differences in kind among properties naturally come corresponding differences in kind among sentences attributing such properties to objects. Some such sentences (e.g., aesthetic-property-attributing sentences) might well be true only in (say) the verificationist sense. On the other hand, some such sentences (e.g., about macro-physical objects) might well be true only in (say) the correspondence sense, while other kinds of sentences (e.g., about the past) might be true only in the semantic sense or the like.

Of course, if pluralism, along the foregoing lines, is true then each of the other 'monistic' families (viz., correspondence, semantic, verifiability, transparency), while getting part of the full story right, is ultimately refuted; for, the correct answer to the central question requires more than the one property (or, in the case of transparency, at least some explanatory properties) beyond what such theories recognize. But for the pluralist this is a feature rather than a bug, since, according to the pluralist, different kinds of truth are appropriate for different kinds of domain.

A good case study is the verificationist theory of truth. As argued in Section 4.2.1, there are certain domains – such as the aesthetic domain – which, for independent reasons, appear to be socially constructed. Consequently, for these domains, the 'V-schema'

$$\text{`}p\text{' is verifiable if and only if } p$$

is independently plausible. Thus, by analyzing truth as verifiability, we get an explanation of the T-schema for these domains.

However, there are also domains – such as the astrophysical domain and the domain of everyday macroscopic objects – which *do not* have the appearance of being socially constructed. Consequently, the verificationist theory is not a plausible analysis of truth for these domains. By contrast, the semantic theory, correspondence theory and transparency theory *are* plausible analyses of truth for these domains, since they offer explanations of the T-schema.

The advantage of the pluralist theory is that we can have 'the best of both worlds'. For domains which appear socially constructed, such as the aesthetic domain, we can analyze truth as verifiability. On the other hand, for domains which do *not* appear socially constructed, such as the domain of everyday macroscopic objects, we can analyze truth as correspondence to the facts, semantic correctness or transparency. As a result, we can guarantee that the pluralist theory offers an explanation of the T-schema across all domains.

6.3 ARGUMENT FOR THE PLURALITY ANSWER

Arguments for pluralism generally point to problems with the other accounts. Details aside (because sufficiently many details are sketched in preceding chapters), one argument for pluralism is as follows.

(1) All monistic theories of truth are *correct* for some domain of sentences.
(2) All monistic theories of truth are *incorrect* for some domain of sentences.
(3) Only a pluralist theory of truth can be correct over all domains of sentences. [From (1), (2)]
(4) The correct theory of truth is correct over *all* domains of sentences.
(5) Some pluralist theory of truth is correct. [From (3), (4)]

6.4 EVALUATION

There are at least two central lines to evaluate: the argument for the thesis, and the thesis itself. A particular argument may have problems even if the thesis (i.e., the conclusion of the argument) is true.

6.4.1 EVALUATION OF THE ARGUMENT

The strength of the argument turns on the strength of its premises. The strength of the given premises turns on too many issues to cover at length in this discussion; however, one quickly gets a sense of arguments for (1) and (2) by motivations and, respectively, problems for the correspondence answer, semantic answer, verifiability answer and the transparency answer. Insofar as such motivations and would-be problems support (1) and (2), respectively, the first two premises of the argument for pluralism are in good nick. Premise (4), in turn, is well-motivated provided that a theory of truth needs to be a theory of truth *for all sentences*, which is generally assumed in truth studies.

On the whole, the argument is as good as the motivation and support behind its premises. How good that happens to be is a matter for readers to discern.

6.4.2 EVALUATION OF THE ANSWER

We now turn to the evaluation of the pluralist answer itself, independent of the argument given in support of it. We discuss three objections to the pluralist theory.

6.4.2.1 Collapse into Monism

One objection to pluralism concerns its would-be pluralism. Pluralism, on the current sketch, claims that there's no single property that's both common to 'all truths' (whatever that means under pluralism) and makes them all true. Instead, says pluralism, there are at least three – or four, if transparency's 'logical property' counts – properties that answer the central question in different domains. The properties, again, are

- C: correspondence truth
- S: semantic truth
- V: verificationist truth
- TT: transparent truth.

This appears to be a pluralism, since these are very different properties. But given the universal role of disjunction ('or'), presumably there is a single, albeit derivative, property that reduces the given pluralism to monism. Namely, where $\vee$ is disjunction, $\wedge$ is conjunction ('and') and D_C, D_S, D_V, D_{TT} are the domains of the respective correspondence, semantic, verificationist and transparent truth properties:

$$[D_C(x) \wedge C(x)] \vee [D_S(x) \wedge S(x)] \vee [D_V(x) \wedge V(x)]$$
$$\vee [D_{TT}(x) \wedge TT(x)]$$

that is,

- *either* correspondence-true *or* semantic-true *or* verification-true *or* transparent-true.

Given the way disjunction works, this disjunctive property is satisfied by any sentences in the relevant domains that are 'true by correspondence', 'true by semantics', 'true by verifiability' or 'transparent-true'. Hence, any sentence that the would-be pluralist calls *true* is therefore disjunctively true (i.e., true in the sense of the given disjunctive property) *and vice versa*. But, then, the pluralist is really just a monist in the end.

If the would-be non-monistic pluralism that involves all and only the 'disjuncts' of the given disjunctive property is to avoid monism then such a disjunctive property needs to be ruled out. But on what grounds? It's unlikely that there's any non-ad-hoc way of avoiding the given disjunctive property, and hence no non-ad-hoc way of avoiding a monism about truth in the end.

6.4.2.1.1 A Possible Reply   Perhaps the most natural reply is to simply grant the objection, reframing pluralism as a derivative monism that arises from a primitive plurality of truth properties. More precisely, the pluralist should accept that truth, on their view, is best analyzed disjunctively:

(Pluralism) $Tr(x) =_{df} [D_C(x) \wedge C(x)] \vee [D_S(x) \wedge S(x)] \vee [D_V(x) \wedge V($
$[D_{TT}(x) \wedge TT(x)]$.

This disjunctive theory of truth is still a distinct monistic theory of truth that differs from all other (non-derivative) monistic theories of truth.

6.4.2.2 Mixed Compounds

Another objection concerns so-called 'mixed compounds'. Suppose that A is an 'aesthetic sentence' in the sense that it attributes only some aesthetic property to some object, while *B* is some 'biological sentence' in the sense that it attributes only some biological property to some object. If one wishes, for concreteness, one may think of *A* and *B*, respectively, as

- All mountains are very beautiful.
- Salamanders are ectothermic.

Now, the motivation for pluralism suggests that *A* is verification-true while *B* is correspondence-true. This is fine so far as it goes, but now one must consider logical compounds (and beyond). What sort of truth is the disjunction of *A* and *B*? Consider

$$A \lor B$$

Is this correspondence-true or verification-true? Or is it *both* correspondence-true and verification-true? Answers are not obvious. The same question arises for conjunctions (e.g., $A \land B$), and indeed negations of such disjunctions and conjunctions.

The problem is that sentences such as the disjunction (or conjunction, etc.) of *A* and *B*, understood as above, are neither 'biological sentences' nor 'aesthetic sentences' but rather 'mixed compounds' (as the term goes). If 'what makes sentences true' turns on the *kind* of sentence (e.g., its 'domain') then compounds of such sentences must have a *kind*. What that kind may be is not immediately clear.

6.4.2.2.1 A Possible Reply

Rather than attempting to assign a mixed compound to a kind governed by its own type of truth, which seems tenuous at best, a better response for the pluralist is to slightly modify the formulation of pluralism.

The problem of mixed compounds does not pose a problem for atomic sentences – sentences which do not contain logical connectives ('and', 'or', 'not' etc). Consequently, for atomic sentences, the formulation of pluralism remains unchanged. Namely:

(Atomic Plural Truth) $Tr(x) =_{df} [D_C(x) \land C(x)] \lor [D_S(x) \land S(x)] \lor [D_V(x) \land V(x)] \lor [D_{TT}(x) \land TT(x)].$

The difference comes when we consider how to analyze truth for complex sentences – sentences which do *not* contain logical connectives. As we have seen, there is no natural way to divide complex sentences into kinds. Instead, we will borrow some machinery from the semantic theory of truth, and define truth for complex sentences *inductively*. Recall that $\wedge$ stands for conjunction ('and'), $\vee$ stands for disjunction ('or') and $\neg$ stands for negation ('not'). Having defined truth for atomic sentences in an entirely non-circular manner, the pluralist can inductively define truth for conjunctions, disjunctions and negations of conjunctions, disjunctions and negations as follows:

1. $Tr(\ulcorner \varphi \vee \psi \urcorner) =_{df} Tr(\ulcorner \varphi \urcorner)$ or $Tr(\ulcorner \psi \urcorner)$
2. $Tr(\ulcorner \varphi \wedge \psi \urcorner) =_{df} Tr(\ulcorner \varphi \urcorner)$ and $Tr(\ulcorner \psi \urcorner)$
3. $Tr(\ulcorner \neg\neg\varphi \urcorner) =_{df} Tr(\ulcorner \varphi \urcorner)$
4. $Tr(\ulcorner \neg(\varphi \vee \psi) \urcorner) =_{df} Tr(\ulcorner \neg\varphi \urcorner)$ and $Tr(\ulcorner \neg\psi \urcorner)$
5. $Tr(\ulcorner \neg(\varphi \wedge \psi) \urcorner) =_{df} Tr(\ulcorner \neg\varphi \urcorner)$ or $Tr(\ulcorner \neg\psi \urcorner)$.

Consider, for example, the mixed compound

All mountains are very beautiful or salamanders are ectothermic.

By clause 1, this sentence is true if and only if (i) 'All mountains are very beautiful' is true or (ii) 'Salamanders are ectothermic' is true. But now we have reduced the truth of the mixed compound to the truth of two atomic sentences, which can be handled in the standard pluralist way – using the type of truth appropriate for the domain to which each atomic sentence belongs.

More generally, the inductive clauses reduce the truth of compound sentences to the truth of atomic sentences, which can be handled using the pluralist account of atomic truth.

6.4.2.3 Mixed Inferences

A neighboring problem to the problem of mixed compounds involves 'mixed inferences' (as the term is used), wherein a logically valid argument involves a premise of 'one kind' (i.e., from one domain) and another premise or conclusion from a distinct kind (or domain). Examples arising from the examples above:

- Example 1:
  - All mountains are beautiful.
  - Salamanders are ectothermic.
  - Therefore, all mountains are beautiful and Salamanders are ectothermic.
- Example 2:
  - Salamanders are ectothermic.
  - Therefore, either Salamanders are ectothermic or all mountains are beautiful.

The apparent problem for pluralism is that logical validity is generally taken to be 'truth preserving', in the sense that the conclusion is true in any logical possibility in which all premises are true. Validity thereby looks to involve a single property being 'preserved' across logical possibilities; however, there is no *single* property being preserved in the examples, since the various sentences are only 'true' in different senses.

6.4.2.3.1 A Possible Reply   Logical validity is underpinned by the meanings of the logical connectives. For example,

- All mountains are beautiful.
- Salamanders are ectothermic.
- Therefore, all mountains are beautiful and Salamanders are ectothermic.

is logically valid in virtue of the meaning of the logical connective 'and'. Consequently, the solution we gave to the problem of mixed compounds straightforwardly carries over to the problem of mixed inferences.

Consider, for example, the inference above. Suppose 'All mountains are beautiful' and 'Salamanders are ectothermic' are both true in some logical possibility w. Then, by clause 2 of the inductive definition of pluralist truth, 'All mountains are beautiful and salamanders are ectothermic' is also true in w. Thus, the modified pluralist theory explains why the inference is valid.

6.5 CHAPTER SUMMARY

In this chapter, we introduced the pluralist theory of truth, according to which the feature which makes a sentence true varies depending on the domain to which the sentence belongs. We outlined an argument for the pluralist theory on the basis that while all monistic theories of truth surveyed in this book are correct for some domains, no such theory is correct for all domains. We noted the strength of this argument depends on the strength of the motivations for and objections to the various monistic theories of truth surveyed in this text. Finally, we discussed some objections to the pluralist theory of truth – in particular, the collapse problem, the problem of mixed compounds and the problem of mixed inferences.

NOTES

21. We repeat here that we are herein only giving a representative idea of the target family of pluralist views, focusing on the distinctive difference between it and other theories discussed in this book. Some pluralists think that there is one property that answers the question but it's a 'multiply realizable' or 'functional' or some such property. We skip over the subtleties of all this here, leaving details to further reading.

22. As throughout the book, we are not in any way endorsing such observations, but simply discussing them as possible motivation for some sort of pluralism.

FURTHER READING

- Historical background: Hilary Putnam, 'Sense, Nonsense, and the Senses: An Inquiry into the Powers of the Human Mind,' *Journal of Philosophy*, Vol. 91, pp. 445–515.
- Classic work: Crispin Wright, *Truth and Objectivity* (Harvard University Press: Cambridge, MA, 1992).
- Contemporary discussion:
  - Michael Lynch, *Truth in Context: An Essay on Objectivity and Pluralism* (MIT Press: Cambridge, MA, 1998).
  - Nikolaj J. L. L. Pedersen and Cory Wright (eds.), *Truth and Pluralism: Current Debates* (Oxford University Press: New York, 2013).

PARADOX

7.1 INTRODUCTION

In the previous five chapters, we evaluated five different accounts of the nature of truth: the correspondence theory, the semantic theory, the verificationist theory, the transparency theory and the pluralist theory. By contrast, in this final chapter we do not evaluate a particular theory of truth, but rather discuss a challenge to the very possibility of developing an adequate theory of truth. This challenge is the liar paradox.

As we saw in Section 1.3.8, the liar paradox arises when we attempt to build a theory of truth which applies to *every* sentence of English, including those sentences which themselves contain the predicate 'is true'. Consequently, until this point, we restricted our attention to just the 'true'-free part of English. But if we want our theory of truth to be complete – regardless of whether that theory is the correspondence, semantic, verificationist, transparency or pluralist theory – we must eventually face up to the challenge of extending our theory beyond this fragment. In this chapter, we take the initial steps towards answering the challenge.

DOI: 10.4324/9781003190103-7

7.2 THE LIAR, MORE PRECISELY

We begin by re-introducing the liar paradox. In order to understand the liar, we need to make explicit exactly which assumptions underlie the paradox. This requires introducing some concepts which are more abstract than those previously discussed in the book. Since this is an introductory book, we try to keep the technicalities to a minimum. Nevertheless, to do the liar justice, some technicalities will be required.

7.2.1 ENTAILMENT

Let $\mathcal{T}$ be a theory of some domain. In essence, $\mathcal{T}$ is just a collection of sentences. For example, if $\mathcal{T}$ is the correspondence theory of truth then $\mathcal{T}$ is a collection of sentences such as:

- Every true sentence corresponds to a fact.
- A sentence of the form 'p or q' corresponds to a fact Φ if and only if 'p' corresponds to Φ or 'q' corresponds to Φ.
- For any facts Φ and Ψ, there exists a compound fact $\Phi + \Psi$ composed of Φ and Ψ.
- ...

For most theories, the sentences contained in the theory do not exhaust the information content of the theory. A theory also has *implicit* information content – sentences any rational theorist who accepts the theory is committed to accepting, even though those sentences do not appear in the formulation of the theory itself. For example, given that the correspondence theory contains 'Every true sentence corresponds to a fact', the implicit information content of the correspondence theory includes 'Every true sentence corresponds to something', since a rational theorist who accepts the first sentence is thereby committed to accepting the second sentence too.

When $\mathcal{T}$ is a theory, we write

$$\mathcal{T} \vDash \varphi$$

to mean that φ is part of either the explicit or implicit information content of $\mathcal{T}$. We refer to $\vDash$ as *entailment*, and say that $\mathcal{T}$ *entails* φ.

Suppose, for example, that $\mathcal{T}$ is the correspondence theory. Since $\mathcal{T}$ contains the sentence 'Every true sentence corresponds to a fact', we have

$$\mathcal{T} \vDash \text{every true sentence corresponds to a fact.}$$

But, in addition, since 'Every true sentence corresponds to something' is part of the implicit information content of $\mathcal{T}$, we also have

$$\mathcal{T} \vDash \text{every true sentence corresponds to something.}$$

In general, if $\mathcal{T}$ contains the sentence φ then $\mathcal{T} \vDash \varphi$. But since theories usually have a great deal of non-explicit information content, there are likely many sentences ψ such that $\mathcal{T} \vDash \psi$ even though ψ is not contained in $\mathcal{T}$.

7.2.2 LIAR INGREDIENTS

The liar paradox has three ingredients. Each ingredient is a principle governing $\vDash$. In this section, we outline these three ingredients and explain why they are plausible.

7.2.2.1 T-equivalence

The first ingredient of the liar paradox concerns truth in particular:[23]

(T-equivalence) Suppose $\mathcal{T}$ contains an adequate theory of truth. Then $\mathcal{T} \vDash Tr(\ulcorner \varphi \urcorner)$ if and only if $\mathcal{T} \vDash \varphi$.

T-equivalence asserts that any theory containing an adequate theory of truth should not distinguish between the truth of $Tr(\ulcorner \varphi \urcorner)$ and the truth of φ. This is plausible because the T-schema

$$\text{`}p\text{' is true if and only if } p$$

seems to be the essential feature of truth. Thus, since any adequate theory of domain D should capture the essential features of D, any theory which contains an adequate theory of truth should capture the (material) equivalence between $Tr(\ulcorner \varphi \urcorner)$ and φ.

7.2.2.2 Indiscernability of Identicals

The second ingredient of the liar paradox concerns identity. In ordinary English, 'identity' has a number of different meanings. Here we are concerned with one meaning in particular – so-called *numerical* identity. This sense of 'identity' is usually expressed using $=$, and simply means that the objects it is applied to are one and the same. For example, $2 + 2 = 4$ because the number on the left (the result of adding 2 to itself) *just is* the number on the right – they are one and the same object.

To state the second ingredient of the liar, let $\varphi(a)$ be a sentence containing the name a and $\varphi(b)$ be the sentence obtained from $\varphi(a)$ by replacing the name a with the name b. For example, if a is 'Muhammad Ali', b is 'Cassius Clay' and $\varphi(a)$ is 'Muhammad Ali won the world heavyweight championship in 1964' then $\varphi(b)$ is the sentence 'Cassius Clay won the world heavyweight championship in 1964'. The second ingredient can now be stated as follows:

(Indiscernability of Identicals)   Suppose $\mathcal{T}$ contains $a = b$. Then $\mathcal{T} \vDash$
$\phi(a)$ if and only if $\mathcal{T} \vDash \phi(b)$.

The indiscernability of identicals (or *IId* for short) asserts that a theory containing $a = b$ cannot make any distinctions between a and b – anything the theory says about a, the theory must also say about b. This is plausible because if a and b really *are* the same object then they must have the very same properties. For example, since Muhammad Ali and Cassius Clay are the very same individual, anything true of Muhammad Ali is also true of Cassius Clay. In particular, since it is true that Muhammad Ali won the world heavyweight championship in 1964, it is also true that Cassius Clay won the world heavyweight championship in 1964.

7.2.2.3 Reductio ad Absurdum

The third and final ingredient of the liar paradox concerns *negation* – 'not' – which we symbolize as $\neg$. Reductio ad absurdum (or *reductio* for short) asserts that if adding φ to a theory results in the theory entailing $\neg\varphi$ then the theory, by itself, already entails $\neg\varphi$. More precisely:

(Reductio ad Absurdum)   If $\mathcal{T} + \varphi \vDash \neg\varphi$ then $\mathcal{T} \vDash \neg\varphi$.

Reductio is the most subtle ingredient of the liar paradox, and so requires careful motivation. Suppose accepting $\mathcal{T} + \varphi$ commits us to accepting $\neg\phi$. Then accepting $\mathcal{T} + \varphi$ commits us to accepting the contradiction formed by φ and $\neg\varphi$. A contradiction cannot possibly be true. Thus, accepting $\mathcal{T} + \varphi$ commits us to accepting an impossibility. Since it is irrational to be committed to accepting an impossibility, it is irrational to accept $\mathcal{T} + \varphi$. Hence, accepting $\mathcal{T}$ commits us to *rejecting* φ. For a rational person, rejecting φ is equivalent to accepting $\neg\varphi$. Consequently, accepting $\mathcal{T}$ commits us to accepting $\neg\varphi$.

7.2.3 THE LIAR PARADOX

With the three ingredients of the liar in place, we are ready to construct the paradox. Let l denote the sentence $\neg Tr(l)$. Then, presumably, $l = \ulcorner \neg Tr(l) \urcorner$ is true, since l and $\ulcorner \neg Tr(l) \urcorner$ refer to one and the same sentence. We will show that any adequate theory of truth which explicitly recognizes the existence of the liar sentence entails a contradiction. More precisely, when $\mathcal{T}$ is an adequate theory of truth, we will show that the theory $\mathcal{T}^*$ obtained by adding $l = \ulcorner \neg Tr(l) \urcorner$ to $\mathcal{T}$ entails both $Tr(l)$ and $\neg Tr(l)$:

1. $\mathcal{T}^* + Tr(l) \vDash Tr(l)$ [by definition of $\vDash$]
2. $\mathcal{T}^* + Tr(l) \vDash Tr(\ulcorner \neg Tr(l) \urcorner)$ [from 1 by IId]
3. $\mathcal{T}^* + Tr(l) \vDash \neg Tr(l)$ [from 2 by T-equivalence]
4. $\mathcal{T}^* \vDash \neg Tr(l)$ [from 3 by reductio]
5. $\mathcal{T}^* \vDash Tr(\ulcorner \neg Tr(l) \urcorner)$ [from 4 by T-equivalence]
6. $\mathcal{T}^* \vDash Tr(l)$ [from 5 by IId]

Note that lines 4 and 6 create the contradiction.

7.2.4 THE UPSHOT

When a theory entails a contradiction, we say that the theory is *inconsistent*. What the liar seems to show is that any attempt to construct an adequate theory of truth is doomed to collapse into inconsistency, *once we combine the theory with seemingly mundane syntactic facts.*

Supposing, as we ordinarily do, that it is irrational to accept an inconsistent theory, this seems to entail there is in fact no adequate theory of truth. But surely this cannot be! Truth, it would seem, is a real and important property, and so there must exist *some* adequate theory as to its nature.

It is helpful to break this argument down into explicit premises:

(1) For any adequate theory of truth $\mathcal{T}$, $\mathcal{T} + l = \ulcorner \neg Tr(l) \urcorner$ is inconsistent [by the liar paradox].
(2) No inconsistent theory is rationally acceptable.
(3) For any adequate theory of truth $\mathcal{T}$, $\mathcal{T} + l = \ulcorner \neg Tr(l) \urcorner$ is not rationally acceptable [from (1), (2)].
(4) $l = \ulcorner \neg Tr(l) \urcorner$ is known to be true.
(5) If combining a theory $\mathcal{T}$ with our knowledge produces a rationally unacceptable theory then $\mathcal{T}$ is not an adequate theory.

---

(6) No theory of truth is adequate [from (3), (4), (5)].

In order to avoid the conclusion, we must reject one of premises (1), (2), (4), (5). But premise (5) merely states that our knowledge should constrain which theories are adequate. This strikes us a beyond rebuke: once we discover that a theory is incompatible with what we know to be true, the theory ought to be rejected. Therefore, the only reasonable response to the argument is to reject one of premises (1), (2), (4).

As we saw in the previous section, premise (1) is supported by three further principles: T-equivalence, the indiscernability of identicals and reductio ad absurdum. Consequently, rejecting premise (1) requires rejecting one of these three liar ingredients. By contrast, rejecting (2) or (4) is compatible with accepting the three liar ingredients. The solutions to the liar therefore fall into two general classes: solutions which accept the liar ingredients, and solutions which reject the liar ingredients. We discuss each class in turn.

7.3 SOLUTIONS WHICH ACCEPT THE LIAR INGREDIENTS

If we choose to continue accepting the liar ingredients then we must either reject premise (2), thereby accepting that an inconsistent theory could be rationally acceptable, or else reject premise (4), thereby rejecting that we know the liar sentence to be self-referential. We discuss each option in turn.

7.3.1 REJECT SELF-REFERENCE

The first solution is to reject (4): perhaps we do not in fact know that $l = \ulcorner \neg Tr(l) \urcorner$ is true. The most straightforward way to argue for this is to argue that, contrary to appearances, $l = \ulcorner \neg Tr(l) \urcorner$ simply fails to be true.

Why are we inclined to accept $l = \ulcorner \neg Tr(l) \urcorner$? Ordinarily, we tend to suppose we can assign a name to anything we want. The sentence

$$\neg Tr(l)$$

is a syntactic object which exists — there it is right above these words! And we can call that object whatever we wish – we can call it *Bob*, we can call it *The Sentence*, we can call it *l*. And if we decide to call the sentence *l* then $l = \ulcorner \neg Tr(l) \urcorner$ automatically becomes true.

Now suppose that, despite the apparent obviousness of everything said above, we conclude from the liar paradox that we are simply wrong about our being able to assign a name to anything we want. On this view, when we try to assign the name *l* to the sentence $\neg Tr(l)$, we somehow fail to do so – perhaps because some 'anti-paradox force field' steps in to prevent the assignment from working. As a result, $l = \ulcorner \neg Tr(l) \urcorner$ fails to be true. But if $l = \ulcorner \neg Tr(l) \urcorner$ fails to be true then there is no need for a theory of truth to be compatible with $l = \ulcorner \neg Tr(l) \urcorner$.

7.3.1.1 Indirect Self-Reference

Unfortunately, banning the kind of *direct* self-reference which arises from assigning l to $\neg Tr(l)$ does not eliminate *all* forms of self-reference. This is because self-reference can also arise *in*directly.

Imagine you have a whiteboard on which you sometimes write various sentences. Consider the sentence

(k)   No sentence on the whiteboard is true.

k is a perfectly well-formed sentence, which in various circumstances is unproblematically true. For example, suppose the only sentence written on the whiteboard is

$$2 + 2 = 3.$$

Then, since $2 + 2 \neq 3$, everyone would agree k is unproblematically true. Thus, there is no *intrinsic* problem with k. Since k might be true, k is a meaningful statement about the world.

Now suppose that, by chance, the only sentence written on the whiteboard is

No sentence on the whiteboard is true.

Then k indirectly asserts of itself that it is not true – and we can use this fact to re-run the liar paradox.[24] Therefore, rejecting self-reference is not a viable solution in general.

7.3.2   ACCEPT THE CONTRADICTION

The second way to solve the liar while holding onto the three liar ingredients is to allow that inconsistent theories may sometimes be rationally acceptable – in particular, allow that the theory $\mathcal{T}^*$ obtained by adding $l = \ulcorner \neg Tr(l) \urcorner$ to $\mathcal{T}$ is rationally acceptable, despite entailing a contradiction.

Why do we ordinarily suppose that inconsistent theories are *not* rationally acceptable? The standard argument is as follows:

(1) A contradiction could not possibly be true.
(2) It is irrational to be committed to accepting something which could not possibly be true.
(3) It is irrational to be committed to accepting a contradiction. [From (1), (2)]
(4) Accepting an inconsistent theory commits us to accepting a contradiction.

---

(5) It is irrational to accept an inconsistent theory. [From (3), (4)]

Premise (2) strikes us as beyond rebuke: we should never be committed to accepting an impossibility. But premise (4) follows directly from the definition of an inconsistent theory. Consequently, to allow for the possibility of an inconsistent theory being rationally acceptable, we must reject premise (1). We must allow that, at least in some circumstances, a contradiction could be true. In particular, given that we accept the three ingredients of the liar, we must accept that both $Tr(l)$ and $\neg Tr(l)$ are *in fact* true. A position according to which some sentence is both true and false (i.e., a true contradiction or 'glut') is a *glut-theoretic position*, where *gluts* are simply 'gluts of truth and falsity' (the dual of 'truth value gaps').[25]

7.3.2.1 The Objection from Common Sense

The simplest objection to a glut-theoretic account is simply that it clashes with common sense. If a house is painted blue then surely it could not also be *not painted blue*. If the Frankie the dog is sleeping then surely Frankie could not also be *not sleeping*. If a chair is round then surely it could not also be *not round*. In general, a property F is incompatible with its negation $\neg F$.

The standard glut-theoretic response to this simple objection is that common sense is trained on a variety of cases where, indeed, there could be no contradictions. *Being blue* and *not being blue*, *sleeping* and *not sleeping*, *being round* and *not being round*, and so on, are in fact incompatible properties. However, this does not entail that *all* contradictory properties are incompatible. There may be edge cases, such as truth, which are compatible with their negations, and common sense is simply not used to dealing with such edge cases.[26]

7.3.2.2 The Problem of Explosion

There is a problem for the standard glut-theoretic response to the objection from common sense. Given further plausible constraints on $\vDash$, it can be shown that an inconsistent theory will *explode*, in the sense that it entails *every* sentence. Thus, the glut theorist's attempt to contain contradictions to just a few edge cases, such as the liar sentence, is doomed to failure: just adding one contradiction to your theory forces you to add every other contradiction too!

Just two principles are required for explosion. The first is the principle of disjunction introduction (or *DI* for short):

(Disjunction Introduction) If $\mathcal{T} \vDash \varphi$ then, for any ψ, $\mathcal{T} \vDash \varphi \lor \psi$ (likewise $\mathcal{T} \vDash \psi \lor \varphi$).[27]

Disjunction introduction is justified by the nature of 'or': for $\varphi \lor \psi$ to be true *just is* for at least one of φ, ψ to be true. Hence, if a theory is committed to the truth of φ then the theory is automatically committed to the truth of $\varphi \lor \psi$ (likewise $\psi \lor \varphi$).

The second principle is the principle of disjunctive syllogism (or *DS* for short):

(Disjunctive Syllogism) If $\mathcal{T} \vDash \varphi \lor \psi$ (likewise $\mathcal{T} \vDash \psi \lor \varphi$) and $\mathcal{T} \vDash \neg\varphi$ then $\mathcal{T} \vDash \psi$.

The justification for disjunctive syllogism is more subtle than the justification for disjunction introduction. Suppose that accepting $\mathcal{T}$ commits us to accepting both $\varphi \lor \psi$ and $\neg\varphi$. Accepting $\neg\varphi$ is, for a rational person, equivalent to *rejecting* φ. Thus, accepting $\mathcal{T}$ commits us to accepting $\varphi \lor \psi$ and rejecting φ. But if we accept $\varphi \lor \psi$ then we accept that the world is either in a φ-state or a ψ-state. Since we reject that the world is in a φ-state, only one option remains – the world must be in a ψ-state!

From disjunction introduction and disjunctive syllogism we can prove explosion:

(Explosion)   If $\mathcal{T} \vDash \varphi$ and $\mathcal{T} \vDash \neg\varphi$ then, for any ψ, $\mathcal{T} \vDash \psi$.

The proof is straightforward. Suppose $\mathcal{T} \vDash \varphi$ and $\mathcal{T} \vDash \neg\varphi$. Let ψ be any sentence whatsoever. Since $\mathcal{T} \vDash \varphi$, we have by disjunction introduction that $\mathcal{T} \vDash \varphi \vee \psi$. But then, since $\mathcal{T} \vDash \neg\varphi$, we have by disjunctive syllogism that $\mathcal{T} \vDash \psi$.

In particular, let $\mathcal{T}$ be an adequate theory of truth and $\mathcal{T}^*$ be the result of adding $l = \ulcorner \neg Tr(l) \urcorner$ to $\mathcal{T}$. Then, by explosion, we have

$\mathcal{T}^* \vDash$ A purple dragon lives in the basement of the United States

Capitol.

Clearly, however, no reasonable person would accept a theory which entails the existence of dragons in the Capitol.

7.3.2.2.1 A Possible Reply
What we have shown is that, in order to have a viable glut-theoretic response to the liar, the glut theorist must reject either disjunction introduction or disjunctive syllogism. Since disjunction introduction falls directly out of the meaning of 'or', it is not a promising candidate for rejection. Consequently, glut theorists typically reject disjunctive syllogism. This requires the glut theorist to identify where the justification for disjunctive syllogism goes wrong.

For glut theorists, the derivation of disjunctive syllogism goes wrong by assuming that acceptance of $\neg\varphi$ is rationally equivalent to rejection of φ. Why believe that accepting $\neg\varphi$ is rationally equivalent to rejecting φ? The equivalency can be justified in two parts.

- Suppose, as we ordinarily do, that at most one of φ and $\neg\varphi$ can be true. Then accepting φ is rationally incompatible with accepting $\neg\varphi$. Thus, accepting $\neg\varphi$ requires us to reject φ.
- Suppose, as we ordinarily do, that at least one of φ and $\neg\varphi$ must be true. Then rejecting φ requires us to accept $\neg\varphi$.

Clearly, a glut theorist does not accept the first component of this justification. For glut theorists, φ and $\neg\varphi$ *could* – at least for *some* φ – be true together, and hence accepting $\neg\varphi$ does not require a rational theorist to reject φ. As a result, the justification for disjunctive syllogism does not hold up if, with glut theorists, one recognizes the relevant possibility of gluts.

7.4 SOLUTIONS WHICH REJECT A LIAR INGREDIENT

We now turn to solutions to the liar paradox which choose to reject one of the three liar ingredients: T-equivalence, the identity of indiscernibles and reductio ad absurdum. The identity of indiscernibles – which, recall, states that numerically identical objects have the same properties – is generally taken to be beyond reproach. Thus, the viable options are to either reject T-equivalence, thereby reforming our common sense understanding of truth, or else reject reductio ad absurdum. We discuss each option in turn.

7.4.1 REFORM TRUTH

The principle of T-equivalence states that any adequate theory of truth is committed to the truth of 'p' being materially equivalent to the condition that p. More precisely:

(T-equivalence)   Suppose $\mathcal{T}$ contains an adequate theory of truth. Then $\mathcal{T} \vDash Tr(\ulcorner \phi \urcorner)$ if and only if $\mathcal{T} \vDash \varphi$.

Almost everyone agrees T-equivalence holds when restricted to sentences which do not themselves contain any truth-related notions. The problems arise when we take T-equivalence to hold *unrestrictedly* – including cases, such as the liar sentence, where the sentence in question contains the truth predicate itself. In this section, we consider two solutions to the liar which avoid the contradiction by restricting T-equivalence to only a subset of sentences. Since these solutions alter our ordinary conception of truth – which is underpinned by the universal applicability of T-equivalence – we refer to them as *reformist* solutions.

7.4.1.1 The Tarskian Hierarchy

The first reformist solution is due to the Polish philosopher and logician Alfred Tarski. According to Tarski, the lesson of the liar paradox is that no language $\mathcal{L}$ can contain a predicate which expresses the property of *being a true sentence of* $\mathcal{L}$. Instead, to express the property of being a true sentence of $\mathcal{L}$, we have to ascend to an extended language $\mathcal{L} + Tr_0$, where Tr_0 is a new predicate explicitly introduced to express the property of being a true sentence of $\mathcal{L}$. In turn, if we want to express the property of being a true sentence of $\mathcal{L} + Tr_0$, we have to ascend to an extended language $\mathcal{L} + Tr_0 + Tr_1$, where Tr_1 is a new predicate explicitly introduced to express the property of being a true sentence of $\mathcal{L} + Tr_0$. Continuing on, to express the property of being a true sentence of $\mathcal{L} + Tr_0 + Tr_1$, we have to ascend to $\mathcal{L} + Tr_0 + Tr_1 + Tr_2$. And so on. This series of ever expanding languages

$$\mathcal{L}, \mathcal{L} + Tr_0, \mathcal{L} + Tr_0 + Tr_1, \mathcal{L} + Tr_0 + Tr_1 + Tr_2, \ldots$$

is referred to as the *Tarskian hierarchy*.

How does Tarski's solution apply to English? According to Tarski, the English predicate 'is true' is attempting to do something impossible: it is attempting to express the property of being a true sentence of the very language in which it is contained. Since it is impossible to accomplish this task, 'is true' needs to be replaced by the hierarchy of predicates

'is true$_0$', 'is true$_1$', 'is true$_2$',...

where 'is true$_0$' means *is a true sentence of the 'true'-free fragment of English*, 'is true$_1$' means *is a true sentence of the 'true'-free fragment of English plus 'is true$_0$'*, 'is true$_2$' means *is a true sentence of the 'true'-free fragment of English plus 'is true$_0$' and 'is true$_1$'*, and so on.

Since 'Snow is white' belongs to the 'true'-free fragment of English, expressing the truth of 'Snow is white' in Tarskian English only requires ascending to level 1 of the Tarskian hierarchy (the 'true'-free fragment of English plus 'is true$_0$'):

(S_0) 'Snow is white' is true$_0$.

On the other hand, to express the truth of S_0, we have to ascend to at least level 2:

(S_1) S_0 is true$_1$.

Likewise, to express the truth of S_1, we have to ascend to at least level 3:

(S_2) S_1 is true$_2$.

And so on.

How does Tarski's solution resolve the liar paradox? In Tarskian English, the principle of T-equivalence is replaced by the principle T_k-equivalence for every level k of the Tarskian hierarchy:

(T_k-equivalence)   Suppose $\mathcal{T}$ contains an adequate theory of truth. Then $\mathcal{T} \vDash Tr_k(\ulcorner \phi \urcorner)$ if and only if $\mathcal{T} \vDash \varphi$ for every sentence φ on level of k of the Tarskian hierarchy.

Thus, every instance of T_k-equivalence is restricted to a subset of sentences: those sentences which do not contain Tr_i for any $i \geq k$.

Reconsider the liar sentence

(l) $\neg Tr(l)$.

Since Tr lacks an index, the liar sentence is not a grammatical sentence of Tarskian English. Thus, to make l grammatical, we would need to select an index. Letting k be the index, the liar sentence in Tarskian English is as follows:

(l) $\neg Tr_k(l)$.

Note that, since l contains Tr_k, l belongs to levels $k+1$ and above of the Tarskian hierarchy, but does not belong to any level below $k+1$. In particular, l does not belong to level k. As a result, Tarski's theory entails that l is not true$_k$. That is, if we let $\mathcal{T}$ be Tarski's theory of truth and let $\mathcal{T}^*$ be the result of adding $l = \ulcorner \neg Tr_k(l) \urcorner$ to $\mathcal{T}$ then we have

$$\mathcal{T}^* \vDash \neg Tr_k(l).$$

Following the pattern of the liar derivation, we would go on derive a contradiction from Tarski's theory as follows:

1. $\mathcal{T}^* \vDash \neg Tr_k(l)$ [from Tarski's theory].
2. $\mathcal{T}^* \vDash Tr_k(\ulcorner \neg Tr_k(l) \urcorner)$ [from 1 by T_k-equivalence].
3. $\mathcal{T}^* \vDash Tr_k(l)$ [from 2 by IId].

The problem is that, since l belongs to level $k+1$, line 2 is not in fact a legitimate application of T_k-equivalence! Instead, to express the truth of l we need to ascend to at least level $k+2$:

1. $\mathcal{T}^* \vDash \neg Tr_k(l)$ [from Tarski's theory].
2. $\mathcal{T}^* \vDash Tr_{k+1}(\ulcorner \neg Tr_k(l) \urcorner)$ [from 1 by T_{k+1}-equivalence].
3. $\mathcal{T}^* \vDash Tr_{k+1}(l)$ [from 2 by IId].

But now there is no contradiction − all we have shown is that the liar sentence is not a true sentence on level k (since the liar sentence does not even belong to level k), but *is* a true sentence on level $k+1$, which is not paradoxical.

7.4.1.1.1 The Generalization Problem   As argued in Chapter 5, one of the primary benefits of having a truth predicate is that it enables us to make generalizations. Suppose, for example, that I want endorse everything Professor Jones said last night. Without the truth predicate I would have to recall exactly which sentences Professor Jones uttered − say, $\varphi_1, \varphi_2, \varphi_3, \dots, \varphi_{50}$ − and then assert each of these sentences one by one. Clearly, this is extremely impractical. By contrast, if I have the truth predicate at my disposal then I can simply assert 'Everything Professor Jones said last night is true'.

The principle problem for Tarski's theory is that, if we were to replace 'is true' with the hierarchy of truth predicates

$$\text{'is true}_0\text{', 'is true}_1\text{', 'is true}_2\text{',}\dots$$

then this would substantially hinder our ability to make these kinds of generalizations. This is because, in order to ensure that 'Everything Professor Jones said last night is true$_k$' is in fact equivalent to $\varphi_1, \varphi_2, \varphi_3, \dots, \varphi_{50}$, we would need to ensure that the index k is greater than the index on any truth predicate which occurs in $\varphi_1, \varphi_2, \varphi_3, \dots, \varphi_{50}$. As a result, we would need to *remember* exactly which indices Professor Jones used, which in many circumstances we would be unable to do.

If we cannot remember exactly which indices Professor Jones used, the next best option would be to choose an extremely high index – one high enough to almost certainly be higher than the indices Professor Jones used. Say, Tr_{100}. The problem is that Professor Jones is equally incentivized to choose extremely high indices, so that they can ensure *their* truth-based generalizations work as intended. So, in practice, it is doubtful anyone will ever have any degree of certainty that they have chosen their index high enough to make their generalization work.

7.4.1.2 The Grounding Solution

Unlike Tarski's solution, the second reformist solution to the liar paradox does not suggest replacing 'is true' with a hierarchy of truth predicates. Instead, the second reformist solution partitions sentences into two classes: the *grounded* sentences and the *ungrounded* sentences. According to the second solution, the ungrounded sentences, which include paradoxical sentences such as the liar, are semantically defective, in the sense that they fail to make a contentful claim about reality. As a result, our ordinary ways of reasoning about truth break down for ungrounded sentences. In particular, T-equivalence fails to hold for ungrounded sentences. Call this solution the *grounding solution*. In order to make the grounding solution precise, we need to precisely characterize the conditions under which a sentence containing the truth predicate is grounded.

Consider the sentence $Tr(s)$, where s refers to 'Snow is white'. How do we determine whether $Tr(s)$ is true? We do so by *first* determining the truth-status of s: if s is true then $Tr(s)$ is true, if s is not true then $Tr(s)$ is not true. Consequently, since s refers to 'Snow is white', the problem of determining whether $Tr(s)$ is true reduces to the problem of determining whether 'Snow is white' is true, which reduces to the problem of determining whether snow is white. We can picture this process of evaluation as follows:

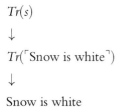

$$Tr(s)$$
$$\downarrow$$
$$Tr(\ulcorner \text{Snow is white} \urcorner)$$
$$\downarrow$$

Snow is white

As another example, consider the sentence $Tr(\ulcorner \neg Tr(s) \urcorner)$. In order to determine whether this sentence is true, we first need to determine whether the 'inner sentence' $\neg Tr(s)$ is true. As before, the problem of determining whether $\neg Tr(s)$ is true reduces to the problem of determining whether s is true: if s is true then $\neg Tr(s)$ is not true, if s is not true then $\neg Tr(s)$ is true. Diagrammatically:

$$Tr(\ulcorner \neg Tr(s) \urcorner)$$
$$\downarrow$$
$$\neg Tr(s)$$
$$\downarrow$$
$$\neg Tr(\ulcorner \text{Snow is white} \urcorner)$$
$$\downarrow$$

Snow is white

In general, we determine whether a sentence containing the truth predicate is true by repeatedly stripping off the truth predicate until we reach a sentence which is not itself about truth, whose truth-status we can determine by direct comparison with reality. We say that a sentence is *grounded* when this process of stripping off the truth predicate does in fact result in a 'ground sentence' – a sentence which does not contain the truth predicate.

One of the lessons of the liar paradox is that *not all sentences are grounded*. Reconsider the liar sentence $\neg Tr(l)$, where l refers to $\neg Tr(l)$. In order to determine whether $\neg Tr(l)$ is true, we first need to determine whether l is true. However, l points us right back to $\neg Tr(l)$! Thus, the process of stripping off the truth predicate goes into an infinite loop, and we never reach a ground sentence:

$$\neg Tr(l)$$
$$\downarrow$$
$$\neg Tr(^\ulcorner \neg Tr(l)^\urcorner)$$
$$\downarrow$$
$$\neg Tr(l)$$
$$\downarrow$$
$$\neg Tr(^\ulcorner \neg Tr(l)^\urcorner)$$
$$\downarrow$$
$$\neg Tr(l)$$

...

Therefore the liar sentence is ungrounded.

There are also ungrounded sentences which do not directly refer to themselves. Consider, for example, the sentences $Tr(a)$ and $Tr(b)$, where a refers to $Tr(b)$ and b refers to $Tr(a)$. In order to determine whether $Tr(a)$ is true, we first need to determine whether a is true. Since a refers to $Tr(b)$, the problem of determining whether $Tr(a)$ is true reduces to the problem of determining whether $Tr(b)$ is true. However, to determine whether $Tr(b)$ is true, we first need to determine whether b is true. But since b refers to $Tr(a)$, this takes us back to the beginning! Diagrammatically:

$$Tr(a)$$
$$\downarrow$$
$$Tr(^\ulcorner Tr(b)^\urcorner)$$
$$\downarrow$$
$$Tr(b)$$
$$\downarrow$$
$$Tr(^\ulcorner Tr(a)^\urcorner)$$

$$\downarrow$$
$$Tr(a)$$
$$...$$

Therefore $Tr(a)$ and $Tr(b)$ are both ungrounded.

According to the grounding solution, the ungrounded sentences are semantically defective sentences, which fail to make contentful claims about reality – and, as a result, T-equivalence only applies to grounded sentences. We can express this more precisely as follows. Let $G(x)$ mean that x is grounded. The grounding solution then endorses the following restricted version of T-equivalence:

(GT-equivalence) Suppose $\mathcal{T}$ contains an adequate theory of truth and, in addition, $\mathcal{T} \vDash G(\ulcorner \varphi \urcorner)$. Then $\mathcal{T} \vDash Tr(\ulcorner \varphi \urcorner)$ if and only if $\mathcal{T} \vDash \varphi$.

As discussed above, the liar sentence l is *provably* ungrounded. Consequently, no adequate theory of truth entails $G(l)$. As a result, GT-equivalence does not allow us to apply T-equivalence to the liar sentence – thereby blocking the liar derivation.

7.4.1.2.1 The Problem of Revenge

A major obstacle for the grounding solution is the notorious *revenge paradox*. Like the liar paradox, the revenge paradox shows that, in combination with certain additional principles, GT-equivalence entails that any adequate theory of truth which recognizes the existence of a certain self-referential sentence will be inconsistent. Consequently, the revenge paradox seems to show that the grounding solution leaves us no better off than before.

In the case of the revenge paradox, we obtain the self-referential sentence by letting r denote

$$\neg G(r) \vee \neg Tr(r).$$

Consequently, the revenge sentence r asserts of itself that it is either untrue or ungrounded. In addition to GT-equivalence, the revenge paradox relies on five additional ingredients. We have already introduced three of these ingredients: the indiscernibility of identicals, reductio ad absurdum and disjunction introduction. However, the remaining two ingredients are new.

The first new ingredient is a slightly modified version of disjunctive syllogism:

(Negative DS) If $\mathcal{T} \vDash \neg\varphi \vee \psi$ (likewise $\mathcal{T} \vDash \psi \vee \neg\varphi$) and $\mathcal{T} \vDash \varphi$ then $\mathcal{T} \vDash \psi$.

The motivation for negative DS is similar to the motivation for disjunctive syllogism. Suppose a rational theorist accepts $\neg\varphi \vee \psi$. Then they accept that either the world is in a $\neg\varphi$-state or is in a ψ-state. Suppose, in addition, the theorist accepts φ. Then, since φ and $\neg\varphi$ are incompatible, the theorist must reject that the world is in a $\neg\varphi$-state – and hence accept the world is in a ψ-state. Note this argument relies on the law of non-contradiction – the principle which states φ and $\neg\varphi$ cannot be true together. This principle is rejected by glut theorists. However, proponents of the grounding solution are unlikely to be glut theorists – since, as we saw earlier, glut theorists are able to solve the liar without needing to restrict T-equivalence.

The second new ingredient concerns the nature of *grounding*. Recall that, according to the grounding solution, ungrounded sentences are semantically defective, in the sense that they fail to make contentful claims about reality. Consequently, an adequate theory of truth will only entail sentences which, by the lights of that theory, are grounded. More precisely, the grounding solution appears committed to the following principle:

(G-closure) Suppose $\mathcal{T}$ contains an adequate theory of truth. If $\mathcal{T} \vDash \varphi$ then $\mathcal{T} \vDash G(\ulcorner\varphi\urcorner)$.

G-closure states that any theory which contains an adequate theory of truth should be committed to a sentence *only if* the theory is willing to commit to the sentence being grounded.

We now have all the ingredients we need to run the revenge paradox. Let $\mathcal{T}$ be any adequate theory of truth and let $\mathcal{T}^*$ be the theory obtained by adding $r = \ulcorner\neg G(r) \vee \neg Tr(r)\urcorner$ to $\mathcal{T}$. We will show that $\mathcal{T}^*$ entails both $G(r)$ and $\neg G(r)$, and hence is inconsistent:

1. $\mathcal{T}^* + Tr(r) + G(r) \vDash Tr(r)$ [by definition of $\vDash$]
2. $\mathcal{T}^* + Tr(r) + G(r) \vDash G(r)$ [by definition of $\vDash$]
3. $\mathcal{T}^* + Tr(r) + G(r) \vDash Tr(^\ulcorner \neg G(r) \vee \neg Tr(r)^\urcorner)$ [from 1 by IId]
4. $\mathcal{T}^* + Tr(r) + G(r) \vDash G(^\ulcorner \neg G(r) \vee \neg Tr(r)^\urcorner)$ [from 2 by IId]
5. $\mathcal{T}^* + Tr(r) + G(r) \vDash \neg G(r) \vee \neg Tr(r)$ [from 3, 4 by GT-equivalence]
6. $\mathcal{T}^* + Tr(r) + G(r) \vDash \neg Tr(r)$ [from 2, 5 by negative DS]
7. $\mathcal{T}^* + G(r) \vDash \neg Tr(r)$ [from 6 by reductio]
8. $\mathcal{T}^* + G(r) \vDash \neg G(r) \vee \neg Tr(r)$ [from 7 by DI]
9. $\mathcal{T}^* + G(r) \vDash G(r)$ [by definition of $\vDash$]
10. $\mathcal{T}^* + G(r) \vDash G(^\ulcorner \neg G(r) \vee \neg Tr(r)^\urcorner)$ [from 9 by IId]
11. $\mathcal{T}^* + G(r) \vDash Tr(^\ulcorner \neg G(r) \vee \neg Tr(r)^\urcorner)$ [from 8, 10 by GT-equivalence]
12. $\mathcal{T}^* + G(r) \vDash Tr(r)$ [from 11 by IId]
13. $\mathcal{T}^* + G(r) \vDash \neg G(r)$ [from 8, 12 by negative DS]
14. $\mathcal{T}^* \vDash \neg G(r)$ [from 13 by reductio]
15. $\mathcal{T}^* \vDash \neg G(r) \vee \neg Tr(r)$ [from 14 by DI]
16. $\mathcal{T}^* \vDash G(^\ulcorner \neg G(r) \vee \neg Tr(r)^\urcorner)$ [from 15 by G-closure]
17. $\mathcal{T}^* \vDash G(r)$ [from 16 by IId]

Note that lines 14 and 17 create the contradiction.[28]

7.4.2 REJECT REDUCTIO AD ABSURDUM

In the previous section, we discussed blocking the liar derivation by rejecting T-equivalence. In this section, we discuss the second route to blocking the liar derivation: rejecting reductio ad absurdum.

(Reductio ad Absurdum) If $\mathcal{T} + \varphi \vDash \neg\varphi$ then $\mathcal{T} \vDash \neg\varphi$.

Recall the motivation for reductio. Suppose adding φ to our theory $\mathcal{T}$ commits us to accepting $\neg\varphi$. Then adding φ to $\mathcal{T}$ commits us to accepting the contradiction formed by φ and $\neg\varphi$. A contradiction could not possibly be true. Thus, since it is irrational to be committed to accepting an impossibility, it is irrational to accept $\mathcal{T} + \varphi$. Therefore, so long as we accept $\mathcal{T}$, we must reject φ. But rejecting φ is rationally equivalent to accepting $\neg\varphi$. So accepting $\mathcal{T}$ commits us to accepting $\neg\varphi$.

The key premise in this argument is that rejecting φ is rationally equivalent to accepting $\neg\varphi$. We saw in Section 7.3.2.2.1 that this premise is justified in two parts:

- Suppose, as we ordinarily do, that φ and $\neg\varphi$ cannot be true together. Then accepting φ is rationally incompatible with accepting $\neg\varphi$. Thus, accepting $\neg\varphi$ requires us to reject φ.
- Suppose, as we ordinarily do, that at least one of φ and $\neg\varphi$ must be true. Then rejecting φ requires us to accept $\neg\varphi$.

Glut theorists reject the first part of this justification, since, on their view, a contradiction could in some circumstances be true. However, philosophers who favor solving the liar paradox by dropping reductio generally do not accept glut theory – indeed, many view dropping reductio as a method of solving the paradox *without* resorting to glut theory. (Some philosophers think that some paradoxes are gluts, some 'gaps', and so are not one-response-fits-all theorists. We set this aside here, for simplicity). Consequently, opponents of reductio generally agree that accepting $\neg\varphi$ rationally requires us to reject φ.

By contrast, since the argument for reductio essentially relies on rejection of φ rationally requiring acceptance of $\neg\varphi$, opponents of reductio are forced to reject the second part of the justification. Consequently, opponents of reductio reject the assumption that at least one of φ, $\neg\varphi$ *must* be true. More precisely, opponents of reductio reject the law of excluded middle (or *LEM* for short):

(LEM)   For any φ, $\vDash \varphi \vee \neg\varphi$

where $\vDash \psi$ means that every theory entails ψ. According to the law of excluded middle, reality is completely filled in, with every question decided. As a result, a solution to the liar which rejects the law of excluded middle (and hence rejects reductio) is known as a *gap-theoretic solution*, since it recognizes the existence of truth-value gaps (dual of truth-value gluts).

As we saw in Chapter 4, verificationists already have reason to reject the law of excluded middle: since our methods of forming beliefs about reality fail to settle every possible question, some questions simply fail to have an answer. Proponents of gap-theoretic solutions are not generally verificationists, however. Instead, gap theorists tend to agree with proponents of the grounding solution that ungrounded sentences, such as the liar, fail to make contentful claims about reality. However, instead of restricting T-equivalence to grounded sentences, opponents of reductio instead see 'the law of excluded middle' (and hence reductio) as in fact not a *logical* law but a principle restricted to grounded sentences. Consequently, since we cannot apply reductio to the liar sentence, the liar derivation is blocked.

7.5 A THEORY OF ENTAILMENT

In the previous section, we saw two different routes to solving the liar which rejected constraints on $\vDash$ not specifically related to truth. In order to avoid explosion, the glut-theoretic solution – which takes the liar sentence to be both true and false – rejects disjunctive syllogism:

(Disjunctive Syllogism) If $\mathcal{T} \vDash \varphi \vee \psi$ (likewise $\mathcal{T} \vDash \psi \vee \varphi$) and $\mathcal{T} \vDash \neg\varphi$ then $\mathcal{T} \vDash \psi$.

In contrast, a gap-theoretic solution rejects the law of excluded middle and, consequently, rejects reductio ad absurdum:

(Law of Excluded Middle) For any φ, $\vDash \varphi \vee \neg\varphi$.

(Reductio ad Absurdum) If $\mathcal{T} + \varphi \vDash \neg\varphi$ then $\mathcal{T} \vDash \neg\varphi$.

To properly evaluate these competing solutions, we need to get clearer about the nature of $\vDash$.

The study of the nature of $\vDash$ is the subject matter of *formal logic*. Since this book is an introduction to truth, rather than to formal logic, we do not attempt to give a comprehensive account of $\vDash$ here.[29] We will, however, sketch the outlines of the standard story about $\vDash$, filling in enough detail to see what assumptions about $\vDash$ underpin disjunctive syllogism, the law of excluded middle and reductio ad absurdum.

7.5.1   THE MODEL THEORETIC ANALYSIS

The fundamental idea at the heart of modern formal logic is that entailment is a relation of necessary truth-preservation. More precisely, what it means for $\mathcal{T} \vDash \varphi$ to be true is that φ is true in any logically possible universe in which $\mathcal{T}$ is true. Why is this plausible? Recall that we initially characterized $\vDash$ as follows: $\mathcal{T} \vDash \varphi$ if and only if any rational theorist who accepts $\mathcal{T}$ is thereby committed to accepting φ. Analyzing $\vDash$ as necessary truth-preservation explains *why* we are rationally committed to anything our theory entails: our theory could not be true unless its entailments are also true.

In formal logic, a logically possible universe is called a *model*. Consequently, the standard analysis of entailment is:

(Model Theoretic Analysis) $\mathcal{T} \vDash \varphi =_{df}$ for every model $\mathbb{M}$, if $\mathcal{T}$ is true in $\mathbb{M}$ then φ is true in $\mathbb{M}$.

In order to obtain principles governing $\vDash$ from the model theoretic analysis, we need a theory which explains how the truth of a sentence in a logical possibility is determined. Consequently, you might expect that developing a theory of $\vDash$ requires taking a stand on which of the correspondence, semantic, verificationist, transparency and pluralist theories is the correct theory of truth.

However, it turns out that, with the exception of the verificationist theory, all theories of truth discussed in this book agree on certain core structural features of truth, which are sufficient to develop a comprehensive theory of $\vDash$. We will outline these core structural features for the restricted part of English formed by applying $\wedge$ ('and'), $\vee$ ('or'), $\neg$ ('not') to atomic sentences formed by applying monadic predicates F, G, H,...etc to names a, b, c,...etc.

⋆ ⋆ *Parenthetical note: Entailment for verificationists.* Verificationists do not accept all of the structural features of truth outlined in this chapter. In particular, verificationists do not accept the principles concerning $\neg$. As a result, the account of $\vDash$ endorsed by verificationists does not fit into the framework developed in this chapter. The logic preferred by verificationists is known as *intuitionistic logic*.[30] Since intuitionistic logic contains reductio ad absurdum, the liar paradox is just as much a problem for verificationists as for other truth theorists.

However, the issues which arise for modifying intuitionistic logic to solve the liar paradox are distinct from the issues discussed in this chapter. *End note.* ✶ ✶

7.5.2   STRUCTURAL FEATURES OF TRUTH

Each of the correspondence, semantic, transparency, and pluralist theories (at least the modified version of the pluralist theory outlined in Section 6.4.2.2.1) agrees on the following structural features of truth:

S1. Necessarily, $Tr(\ulcorner \varphi \vee \psi \urcorner)$ if and only if $Tr(\ulcorner \varphi \urcorner)$ or $Tr(\ulcorner \psi \urcorner)$.
S2. Necessarily, $Tr(\ulcorner \varphi \wedge \psi \urcorner)$ if and only if $Tr(\ulcorner \varphi \urcorner)$ and $Tr(\ulcorner \psi \urcorner)$.
S3. Necessarily, $Tr(\ulcorner \neg\neg\varphi \urcorner)$ if and only if $Tr(\ulcorner \varphi \urcorner)$.
S4. Necessarily, $Tr(\ulcorner \neg(\varphi \vee \psi) \urcorner)$ if and only if $Tr(\ulcorner \neg\varphi \urcorner)$ and $Tr(\ulcorner \neg\psi \urcorner)$.
S5. Necessarily, $Tr(\ulcorner \neg(\varphi \wedge \psi) \urcorner)$ if and only if $Tr(\ulcorner \neg\varphi \urcorner)$ or $Tr(\ulcorner \neg\psi \urcorner)$.

Of course, the theories disagree about *why* the equivalences are satisfied. According to the correspondence theory, the equivalences are satisfied in virtue of the nature of correspondence (see Section 2.1.2.2). According to the semantic and modified pluralist theories, the equivalences fall directly out of the inductive definition of truth (see Sections 3.1.2.2 and 6.4.2.2.1). According to the transparency theory, the equivalences are satisfied in virtue of the transparency rule, according to which $Tr(\ulcorner \varphi \urcorner)$ and φ are always intersubstitutable. To see the transparency rule in action, note it is trivially true that

Necessarily, $\varphi \vee \psi$ if and only if φ or ψ.

Thus, by substituting $\varphi \vee \psi$ for $Tr(\ulcorner \varphi \vee \psi \urcorner)$, we get:

Necessarily, $Tr(\ulcorner \varphi \vee \psi \urcorner)$ if and only if φ or ψ.

Substituting φ for $Tr(\ulcorner \varphi \urcorner)$, we get:

Necessarily, $Tr(\ulcorner \varphi \vee \psi \urcorner)$ if and only if $T(\ulcorner \varphi \urcorner)$ or ψ.

Finally, substituting ψ for $Tr(\ulcorner\psi\urcorner)$, we obtain S1:

> Necessarily, $Tr(\ulcorner\varphi \vee \psi\urcorner)$ if and only if $Tr(\ulcorner\varphi\urcorner)$ or $Tr(\ulcorner\psi\urcorner)$.

Similar derivations can be given for S2-S5.

By themselves, principles S1-S5 already pin down certain constraints on $\vDash$. For example, we can derive disjunction introduction from S1 alone:

(Disjunction Introduction) If $\mathcal{T} \vDash \varphi$ then, for any ψ, $\mathcal{T} \vDash \varphi \vee \psi$
(likewise $\mathcal{T} \vDash \psi \vee \varphi$).

To see how, suppose $\mathcal{T} \vDash \varphi$. Let $\mathbb{M}$ be a model in which $\mathcal{T}$ is true. To validate disjunction introduction, we need to show that $\varphi \vee \psi$ (likewise $\psi \vee \varphi$) is also true in $\mathbb{M}$ for any choice of ψ. This is easy! Since $\mathcal{T} \vDash \varphi$, φ is true in any model in which $\mathcal{T}$ is true. So, in particular, φ is true in $\mathbb{M}$. But then, by S1, $\varphi \vee \psi$ (likewise $\psi \vee \varphi$) is true in $\mathbb{M}$ for any ψ.

It turns out, however, that principles S1-S5 alone are not enough to derive all of the principles about $\vDash$ discussed in this chapter. In particular, S1-S5 are not sufficient to derive disjunctive syllogism, the law of excluded middle or reductio ad absurdum − and so S1-S5 are compatible with both the glut-theoretic and gap-theoretic solutions. In order to derive these additional principles about $\vDash$, we need to assume certain structural features regarding the truth of atomic sentences and their negations.

7.5.3 ATOMIC SENTENCES AND THEIR NEGATIONS

Principles S1-S5 guarantee that the truth-statuses of the atomic sentences and their negations collectively determine the truth-status of *every* sentence in the restricted language formed by $\wedge$, $\vee$ and $\neg$. Consider, for example, the sentence

$$\neg(F(a) \vee \neg G(b)).$$

By S4, we have:

Necessarily, $Tr(\ulcorner\neg(F(a) \vee \neg G(b))\urcorner)$ if and only if $Tr(\ulcorner\neg F(a)\urcorner)$ and $Tr(\ulcorner\neg\neg G(b)\urcorner)$.

Then, by S3, we have

Necessarily, $Tr(\ulcorner\neg(F(a) \vee \neg G(b))\urcorner)$ if and only if $Tr(\ulcorner\neg F(a)\urcorner)$ and $Tr(\ulcorner G(b)\urcorner)$.

Thus, determining the truth-statuses of $\neg F(a)$ and $G(b)$ is sufficient to determine the truth-status of $\neg(F(a) \vee \neg G(b))$: if $\neg F(a)$ and $G(b)$ are both true, $\neg(F(a) \vee \neg G(b))$ is true; if either of $\neg F(a)$ and $G(b)$ is untrue then $\neg(F(a) \vee \neg G(b))$ is untrue.

A similar argument can be given for every other sentence formed by repeatedly applying $\wedge$, $\vee$ or $\neg$ to atomic sentences and their negations. Consequently, to know the truth-status of a sentence in a model, it suffices to know the truth-statuses of the atomic sentences and their negations. It follows that a compete account of $\vDash$ (at least for the restricted $\wedge$, $\vee$, $\neg$ fragment of language) can be obtained by adding constraints on the logically possible distributions of truth across atomic sentences and their negations. In the remainder of this section, we outline the constraints required to validate (respectively, invalidate) the various principles concerning $\vDash$ discussed in this chapter. An account of $\vDash$ generated by a choice of such constraints is referred to as a *logic*.

7.5.3.1 FDE

The weakest account of $\vDash$ is obtained by placing *no* constraints on the logically possible distributions of truth across atomic sentences and their negations. This logic is known as *FDE* – and is essentially the account of $\vDash$ we get from the structural conditions S1-S5 alone. As noted earlier, FDE includes disjunction introduction but does not include disjunctive syllogism, reductio ad absurdum or the law of excluded middle.

7.5.3.2 K3

We obtain the logic K3 by placing *only* the following constraint on the logically possible distributions of truth across atomic sentences and their negations:

(Exclusion)   For any atomic sentence $F(a)$, there is no logical possibility in which both $F(a)$ and $\neg F(a)$ are true.

It can be shown that, given S1–S5, exclusion entails *no* contradiction
(even one formed by complex sentences) can be true in a logical
possibility. Thus, exclusion rules out glut theory. As a result, given
S1, K3 contains disjunctive syllogism. For suppose $\mathcal{T} \vDash \varphi \lor \psi$ and $\mathcal{T} \vDash$
$\neg \varphi$. Let $\mathbb{M}$ be a model of $\mathcal{T}$. Then, by the model theoretic analysis,
both $\varphi \lor \psi$ and $\neg \varphi$ are true in $\mathbb{M}$. Consequently, by S1, φ is true in
$\mathbb{M}$ or ψ is true in $\mathbb{M}$. But, since φ and $\neg \varphi$ cannot both be true, φ is
not true in $\mathbb{M}$. This only leaves one option – ψ must be true in $\mathbb{M}$! So
we have shown that $\mathcal{T} \vDash \psi$.

On the other hand, exclusion is compatible with the possibility of
both $F(a)$ and $\neg F(a)$ failing to be true, and so does not validate the
law of excluded middle. As a result, K3 does not contain reductio ad
absurdum. For suppose $\mathcal{T} + \varphi \vDash \neg \varphi$. By exclusion, φ and $\neg \varphi$ cannot
be true together. Consequently, there is no model in which $\mathcal{T} + \varphi$ is
true. But since the law of excluded middle does not hold, φ failing
to be true does not automatically entail $\neg \varphi$ is true. Thus, we do not
in general have $\mathcal{T} \vDash \neg \varphi$, since there may be a model of $\mathcal{T}$ in which
both φ and $\neg \varphi$ fail to be true.

Since the law of excluded middle and reductio ad absurdum fail in
K3, K3 is a common account of logic among gap theorists. Indeed,
a mathematical proof can be given that a theory of truth which satisfies T-equivalence and recognizes the existence of the liar sentence
is consistent in K3. However, analyzing this proof would take us far
beyond the scope of this text.[31]

7.5.3.3 LP

We obtain the logic LP by placing *only* the following constraint on
the logically possible distributions of truth across atomic sentences
and their negations:

(Exhaustion)   For any atomic sentence $F(a)$, there is no logical
possibility in which both $F(a)$ and $\neg F(a)$ fail to be
true.

It can be shown that, given S1-S5, exhaustion entails the law of excluded middle: for any sentence φ (even a complex sentence) and any model $\mathbb{M}$, either φ is true in $\mathbb{M}$ or $\neg\varphi$ is true in $\mathbb{M}$. As a result, LP contains reductio ad absurdum. For suppose $\mathcal{T} + \varphi \vDash \neg\varphi$. Let $\mathbb{M}$ be any model of $\mathcal{T}$. We know that at least one of φ, $\neg\varphi$ is true in $\mathbb{M}$. But if φ is true in $\mathbb{M}$ then, since $\mathcal{T} + \varphi \vDash \neg\varphi$, $\neg\varphi$ is also true in $\mathbb{M}$. So, in either case, $\neg\varphi$ is true in $\mathbb{M}$. Hence $\mathcal{T} \vDash \neg\varphi$.

On the other hand, exhaustion is consistent with $F(a)$ and $\neg F(a)$ both being true. As a result, LP does not contain disjunctive syllogism. For suppose $\varphi \vee \psi$ and $\neg\varphi$ are both true in $\mathbb{M}$. Then at least one of φ, ψ is true in $\mathbb{M}$. But, since φ and $\neg\varphi$ could be true together, the fact that $\neg\varphi$ is true does not rule out the possibility of φ being true and ψ being untrue.

Since disjunctive syllogism fails, there is no clear path in LP from a contradiction to explosion – and, indeed, it can be shown that explosion fails in LP. Consequently, LP is a common (though not at all only) account of logic among glut theorists. Indeed, as in the case of K3, a mathematical proof can be given that a theory of truth which satisfies T-equivalence and recognizes the existence of the liar sentence does not explode in LP (though it does, of course, entail a contradiction!). The proof is similar to the case of K3, but going into details here would take us far beyond the scope of an introductory book.

7.5.3.4 CL

The strongest logic is obtained by adding *both* exclusion and exhaustion: in any logical possibility, *exactly one* of $F(a)$, $\neg F(a)$ is true. The resulting logic is known as CL or *classical logic*. Classical logic is the logic which is standardly taught in introductory logic classes, and is the logic which the vast majority of philosophers consider to be the correct account of $\vDash$ (though this is probably more because that's all they know than a matter of informed reflection). CL contains all of the principles about $\vDash$ discussed in this chapter: it contains disjunctive syllogism, the law of excluded middle, reductio ad absurdum, disjunction introduction and negative DS. Consequently, any theory of truth which satisfies T-equivalence and recognizes the existence of the liar sentence explodes in CL. Thus, the only option for the classical logician is to reject T-equivalence – which leads to the reformist solutions to the liar discussed in Section 7.4.1.

7.5.3.5 The Combinatorial Argument for FDE

In the previous sections, we saw four different accounts of ⊨, obtained by varying the constraints on the logically possible distributions of truth across atomic sentences and their negations. These accounts are: FDE, K3, LP, CL. With each account comes a different solution to the paradox. If CL is accepted, the only option is to weaken the principle of T-equivalence. If K3 is accepted, the best solution is the gap-theoretic solution, according to which the law of excluded middle fails for the liar sentence. If LP is accepted, the best solution is the glut-theoretic solution, according to which the liar sentence is both true and false. If FDE is accepted, we can choose between the gap-theoretic solution and glut-theoretic solution, where *different paradoxical phenomena* might fuel *different solutions*. (E.g., the so-called *truth-teller sentence*, which says of itself nothing more nor less than that it's true, naturally invites a *gappy* treatment, whereby it's a gap, while some liar sentences, which say nothing more nor less than that they're false, naturally invite a *glutty* treatment, whereby they're gluts.)

The problem of solving the liar paradox therefore reduces, in large part, to the problem of determining the correct constraints on the logically possible distributions of truth across atomic sentences and their negations. (In simpler terminology, this is the problem of specifying the universe of *logical possibilities* – the broadest space of possibilities, broader than just *physical possibility*, *metaphysical possibility*, and so on). Can we argue, on independent grounds, for one set of constraints? Here we will discuss one argument, known as the *combinatorial argument*, that the correct answer is FDE.

The argument is simple. Mathematically, there are four possible ways of distributing truth across $F(a)$ and $\neg F(a)$:

$F(a)$	$\neg F(a)$
True	True
True	Untrue
Untrue	True
Untrue	Untrue

At least in the absence of additional argument, it seems that every such combinatorial possibility should be realized by *some* logical possibility – where *logical* possibility is the broadest sort of possibility (so that any other sort of possibility is a logical possibility but not vice versa). Thus, each row of this table should be realized in some model, at least where models model logical possibility (however inadequately they might ultimately do so). But realizing the first row undermines exclusion and realizing the fourth row undermines exhaustion. Consequently, FDE is the correct account of ⊨.

7.5.3.5.1 A Possible Reply Even proponents of FDE do not accept that *every* combinatorial possibility is logically possible. This is because proponents of FDE accept that logical possibility is at least constrained by S1-S5. This rules out some mathematically possible distributions of truth. For example, it rules out the second row of the following table:

$F(a)$	$F(a) \vee G(a)$
True	True
True	Untrue
Untrue	True
Untrue	Untrue

But if we accept *some* constraints on logical possibility, then why not accept the constraints endorsed by K3, LP or CL?

The proponent of the combinatorial argument will likely respond that, unlike the case of $F(a)$ and $\neg F(a)$, there is a principled reason for ruling out row 2 of the disjunction table – namely, the nature of disjunction, as encapsulated in S1. The trouble is that the proponent of K3, LP or CL could say something similar about negation! The proponent of K3 will say that row 1 of the negation table is ruled out by the nature of negation; the proponent of LP will say that row 4 of the negation table is ruled out by the nature of negation; and the proponent of CL will say that both rows 1 and 4 of the negation table are ruled out by the nature of negation. It is not clear that the proponent of the combinatorial argument has the resources available to resolve this stand-off.

★ ★ *Parenthetical note:* Another response by the advocate of the combinatorial argument points to simple, however imprecise, notions of simplicity, symmetry and naturalness. Why should an account of logical consequence, which involves the largest space of possibilities, recognize gluts but not their exact mirror image *gaps*? Likewise, why should logic recognize gaps as possible but not their duals – their mirror images *gluts*? At least the advocate of CL has a reply, namely, by saying that symmetry and naturalness are preserved by recognizing neither gluts nor gaps, but the advocates of K3 and LP don't have such a reply. Ultimately, the important debate may come down to whether CL or FDE is the right account of *logical* consequence. An advocate of FDE sees CL not as logical consequence but as a restriction of logical consequence involved in true theories – such as mathematical theories – that treat gluts and gaps as theoretically impossible. An advocate of CL has to see FDE as simply *logically* impossible or even incoherent. We leave the reader to reflect further on which of the two accounts is correct. *End note.* ⋆ ⋆

7.5.4   THE CONDITIONAL

So far we have only developed an account of entailment for the part of language formed by $\wedge$, $\vee$ and $\neg$. What about 'if...then...', which we symbolize as $\rightarrow$?

We would normally expect $\rightarrow$ to satisfy at least the following laws:

(Reflexivity)   For all φ, $\vDash \varphi \rightarrow \varphi$.[32]

(Modus Ponens)   If $\mathcal{T} \vDash \varphi$ and $\mathcal{T} \vDash \varphi \rightarrow \psi$ then $\mathcal{T} \vDash \psi$.

It turns out that in the logic CL, we can define a connective using $\neg$ and $\vee$ which satisfies both reflexivity and modus ponens:

$$\varphi \rightarrow \psi =_{\text{df}} \neg \varphi \vee \psi.$$

Thus, there is no need to add $\rightarrow$ to CL as a new connective with its own independent logical properties.

By contrast, it turns out that *no* connective definable from $\wedge$, $\vee$, $\neg$ satisfies both reflexivity and modus ponens in LP, K3 or FDE.

Proving this would be beyond the scope of this text. However, in brief, reflexivity fails in K3 and hence in FDE because K3 recognizes the existence of logical possibilities in which *every* sentence – in particular, whatever sentence $\varphi \to \varphi$ turns out to be – is untrue.

In the case of LP, it is possible to define a connective which satisfies reflexivity (namely, $\varphi \to \psi =_{df} \neg\varphi \lor \psi$, since by the law of excluded middle, $\vDash \neg\varphi \lor \varphi$ holds in LP). However, for somewhat technical reasons, no connective which satisfies reflexivity in LP can also satisfy modus ponens.[33]

Since neither LP, K3 nor FDE can define what is normally expected of a conditional, LP, K3 and FDE are incomplete accounts of $\vDash$ (or so one might suggest).[34] Given that neither LP, K3 nor FDE enjoy a conditional that behaves across all logical possibilities as normally expected, glut theorists and gap theorists have invested much time and effort in extending LP and K3 to a language with a new primitive connective $\to$, in which $\to$ satisfies both reflexivity and modus ponens. It turns out that this can be done – and done so that T-equivalence can be maintained – but the task is complex. The reason for the complexity stems from a new paradox which emerges once $\to$ is added to the language, known as the *Curry paradox* after the logician Haskell Curry.

7.5.4.1 The Curry Paradox

The Curry paradox relies on a new principle about $\vDash$. This principle is known as *conditional proof*:

(Conditional Proof) If $\mathcal{T} + \varphi \vdash \psi$ then $\mathcal{T} \vDash \varphi \to \psi$.

We can motivate conditional proof as follows. Suppose adding φ to $\mathcal{T}$ commits us to accepting ψ. Then accepting $\mathcal{T}$ commits us to accepting ψ conditional on φ. For a rational person, accepting ψ conditional on φ is equivalent to accepting $\varphi \to \psi$. Thus, accepting $\mathcal{T}$ commits us to accepting $\varphi \to \psi$.

The Curry derivation has the same general shape as the liar derivation. First we generate a self-referential sentence by assigning c to the sentence

$$Tr(c) \to \bot$$

where $\perp$ stands for any sentence whatsoever – say, 'A purple dragon lives in the basement of the United States Capitol'. We now argue that any adequate theory of truth which recognizes the existence of c entails $\perp$. Consequently, since it is not rational to accept *everything* (in particular, that a purple dragon lives in the basement of the United States Capitol), it seems to follow that there is no adequate theory of truth.

Let $\mathcal{T}$ be an adequate theory of truth and let $\mathcal{T}^*$ be the result of adding $c = \ulcorner Tr(c) \rightarrow \perp \urcorner$ to $\mathcal{T}$. Then, we have:

1. $\mathcal{T}^* + Tr(c) \vDash Tr(c)$ [by definition of $\vDash$]
2. $\mathcal{T}^* + Tr(c) \vDash Tr(\ulcorner Tr(c) \rightarrow \perp \urcorner)$ [from 1 by IId]
3. $\mathcal{T}^* + Tr(c) \vDash Tr(c) \rightarrow \perp$ [from 2 by T-equivalence]
4. $\mathcal{T}^* + Tr(c) \vDash \perp$ [from 1, 3 by modus ponens]
5. $\mathcal{T}^* \vDash Tr(c) \rightarrow \perp$ [from 4 by conditional proof]
6. $\mathcal{T}^* \vDash Tr(\ulcorner Tr(c) \rightarrow \perp \urcorner)$ [from 5 by T-equivalence]
7. $\mathcal{T}^* \vDash Tr(c)$ [from 6 by IId]
8. $\mathcal{T}^* \vDash \perp$ [from 5, 7 by modus ponens]

Since modus ponens strikes many as essential to $\rightarrow$, conditional proof is generally taken to be the culprit in the Curry paradox. However, developing a strong logic of $\rightarrow$ which lacks conditional proof turns out to be tricky. A full discussion of the issues involved would take us beyond the scope of the book. However, see Appendix E for one way of developing a logic of $\rightarrow$ which is compatible with T-equivalence.

7.6 CHAPTER SUMMARY

The liar paradox threatens to show that *no* theory of truth – regardless of whether it is the correspondence, semantic, verificationist, transparency or pluralist theory – can adequately apply to the entirety of language. In this chapter, we undertook a careful study of the liar, exposing exactly which assumptions underlie the paradox. We then discussed four major routes to solving the paradox:

- According to a glut-theoretic solution, the liar sentence is both true and false. We observed that for glut-theoretic solutions to be viable, a non-standard logic is required, so that contradictions do not 'explode'.

- According to Tarski's solution, the truth predicate should be replaced by a hierarchy of ever-broader predicates, 'is $true_0$', 'is $true_1$', 'is $true_2$',...etc. We observed that Tarski's solution hinders truth from playing its vital role in enabling generalizations.
- According to the grounding solution, our ordinary way of reasoning about truth only applies to a privileged subset of sentences – the *grounded* sentences. We observed that the grounding solution faces the revenge paradox, which attempts to turn the machinery of the solution back against itself.
- According to a gap-theoretic solution, the law of excluded middle fails to apply to the liar sentence – and consequently standard entailment behavior (in particular, reductio ad absurdum) fails to be valid over liar sentences.

After outlining these four major solutions, we investigated which assumptions about logical entailment were required to support the glut-theoretic and gap-theoretic solutions respectively. Finally, we discussed the difficulties involved in extending these solutions to the part of language containing the conditional 'if...then...'.

NOTES

23. Recall that $Tr(\ulcorner \varphi \urcorner)$ is the sentence asserting that φ (in quotations) is true.

24. See Appendix D for details.

25. A specific instance of glut theory is the esoteric-sounding 'ism' called 'dialethism', which in addition to recognizing gluts also holds very specific theses about languages and so-called metalanguages. The neologism 'dialethism' (sometimes 'dialetheism') was coined by Graham Priest and Richard Sylvan (formerly Routley), both pioneering figures in glut theory. The first advocate of a glut-theoretic account of paradox was Florencio Asenjo, a mathematician. For recent discussion of origins and terminology, see Jc Beall's review at *Notre Dame Review of Books*, specifically, https://ndpr.nd.edu/reviews/paradoxes-and-inconsistent-mathematics/.

26. There are other responses that distinguish *logical possibility* from *extra-logical impossibility*, where the latter focuses on a proper subspace of the vast and generous former space. But we set these distinctions aside here.

27. Recall that $\vee$ symbolizes 'or'.

28. For further discussion of the revenge paradox, see Andrew Bacon, 'Can the Classical Logician Avoid the Revenge Paradoxes?' *Philosophical Review*, Vol. 124, No. 3, pp. 299–352, 2015.

29. The interested reader may instead consult Jc Beall and Shay Logan, *Logic: The Basics* (Routledge: New York, 2017).

30. See Dirk Van Dalen, 'Intuitionistic Logic', in D. Gabbay and F. Guenthner (eds.), *Handbook of Philosophical Logic Vol. 3* (Springer: Berlin, Heidelberg, 1986, pp. 225 –339).

31. The interested reader should consult Saul Kripke, 'Outline of a Theory of Truth', *The Journal of Philosophy*, Vol. 72, No. 19, pp. 690–716, 1975.

32. Recall that $\vDash \psi$ means that every theory entails ψ (equivalently, ψ is true in every model).

33. See Jc Beall, Thomas Forster, and Jeremy Seligman, 'A Note on Freedom from Detachment in the Logic of Paradox', *Notre Dame Journal of Formal Logic*, Vol. 54, No. 1, pp. 15–20, 2013, https://doi.org/10.1215/00294527-1731353. See too Hartry Field, *Saving Truth From Paradox* (Oxford University Press: Oxford, 2008).

34. Another response, not uncommon, is to note that $\vDash$ is *logical* consequence, which governs very sparse, topic-neutral vocabulary (viz., $\lor$, $\land$, $\neg$ and first-order quantifiers) that, it turns out, has a conditional (viz., defined out of $\lor$ and $\neg$ as $\neg A \lor B$) that accommodates all logical possibilities (gluts, gaps, etc.) and therefore exhibits weaker-than-expected entailment behavior, but the conditional behaves exactly as expected over the restricted space of logical possibilities that exclude gluts and gaps. We leave further discussion for debate elsewhere.

FURTHER READING

- Historical background: Alfred Tarski, 'The Semantic Conception of Truth', *Philosophy and Phenomenological Research*, Vol. 4, No, 3, pp. 341–376, 1944.

- Classic work: Saul Kripke, 'Outline of a Theory of Truth', *The Journal of Philosophy*, Vol. 72, No. 19, pp. 690–716, 1975; Florencio G. Asenjo, 'A calculus of antinomies', *Notre Dame Journal of Formal Logic*, Vol. 7, No. 1, pp. 103–105, 1966; Graham Priest, 'The Logic of Paradox', *Journal of Philosophical Logic*, Vol. 8, No. 1, pp. 219–241, 1979.

- Contemporary discussion: Hartry Field, *Saving Truth From Paradox* (Oxford University Press: Oxford, 2008); Jc Beall, *Spandrels of Truth* (Oxford University Press: Oxford, 2009).

FINAL SCORE CARD

In this book, we introduced and evaluated five answers to the central philosophical question about truth:

(Central Question)   What feature do all and only the truths have in common, which makes them all true?

These five answers are as follows:

- Correspondence theory: x is true $=_{df}$ x corresponds to a fact.
- Semantic theory: x is true $=_{df}$ x is semantically correct.
- Verificationist theory: x is true $=_{df}$ x is verifiable.
- Transparency theory: for 'p' to be true *just is* for it to be the case that p. Consequently, there is no answer to the central question.
- Pluralist theory: different accounts of truth are appropriate for different domains.

In order to be adequate, an answer to the central question should explain the central phenomena associated with truth. *The* central phenomenon associated with truth is the T-schema, which matches every sentence with a truth condition – a worldly condition under which the sentence is, in actual fact, true:

(T-schema)   'p' is true if and only if p.

DOI: 10.4324/9781003190103-8

We saw that the correspondence, semantic, transparency and plural-ist theories are able to explain the T-schema across all domains. By contrast, although the verificationist theory of truth can explain the T-schema in certain domains – domains where, for independent rea-sons, we do not expect the truth of a sentence to come apart from our ability to verify the sentence – the verificationist theory has trouble explaining the T-schema across *all* domains.

In addition to analyzing T-schema behavior, we classified the five theories according to the position they took on the following common-sense features of truth:

(Meaning Sensitivity)   Whether a sentence is true depends on its meaning.

(Responsiveness)   Whether 'p' is true is determined by whether p, and not the other way around.

The five theories can be categorized in terms of these two properties as follows:

	Entails Meaning Sensitivity	Entails Responsiveness
Correspondence	Yes	Yes
Semantic	Yes	Yes
Verificationist	No	No
Transparency	No	No
Pluralist	Maybe	Maybe

Whether pluralism entails meaning sensitivity and responsiveness depends on exactly which properties we take to account for truth in different domains.

Although the verificationist theory does not entail meaning sensi-tivity, it is at least compatible with meaning sensitivity. For example, if (as many verificationists do) we identify the meaning of a sentence with its verification condition, then truth would be meaning sensitive under the verificationist theory.

The fact that the verificationist theory fails to entail responsive-ness is considered by its proponents to be a feature rather than a bug. This is because failing to entail responsiveness is required for the ver-ificationist theory to be compatible with anti-realism about a given domain, according to which truth *constructs*, rather than responds to, that domain – in the sense that for a sentence 'p' in the given domain, p because 'p' is true.

The transparency theory is incompatible with both meaning sensitivity and responsiveness. However, for the same reason that the transparency theory is incompatible with responsiveness, it is also incompatible with anti-realism. For suppose we have

$$p \text{ because '}p\text{' is true.}$$

An application of the transparency rule entails

$$p \text{ because } p$$

which violates the irreflexivity of explanation (the principle according to which nothing can explain itself). Thus, anti-realists should adopt either the verificationist theory of truth or a pluralist theory of truth according to which verificationist truth governs the anti-realist domains.[35]

NOTE

35. Like the correspondence and semantics theories, this would only be a problem for the transparency theory on the (highly controversial) assumption that anti-realism about some domain is correct.

GLOSSARY

Analysis: An analysis of a property F is an attempt to state the feature common to all and only the Fs, which makes them all F.

Anti-realism: In this book, 'anti-realism' refers to the view that the sentences describing a given domain are not true in virtue of how that domain is configured, but rather the configuration of that domain is explained by which sentences describing it are true. In the wider philosophical literature, 'anti-realism' is more generally used to label any view according to which the way a given domain is configured in some way depends on our attitudes towards that domain or on the language we use to describe that domain.

Compositionality: Compositionality is the principle that the meaning of a sentence is determined by the meanings of the words in the sentence and how those words are arranged.

Context sensitivity: A linguistic expression is context sensitive when the object, property or relation denoted by the expression on a given occasion of use depends in a systematic way on the context in which the sentence is used.

Glut theory: Glut theory involves the claim that there are 'gluts' (or 'true contradictions') – i.e., that for some sentence 'p', both 'it is true that p' and 'it is false that p' are true.

Gap theory: Gap theory involves the claim that there are 'gaps' (or 'untrue contradictions') – i.e., that for some sentence 'p', neither 'it is true that p' nor 'it is false that p' are true.

Entailment: A theory entails a sentence when the sentence is true in any logically possible universe in which the theory is true.

Inductive definition: An inductive definition of a property F is a definition which proceeds by first defining, in an entirely non-circular manner, an initial set of objects which have F and then specifies a fixed set of rules by which F can be transferred from one object to another.

Inconsistency: A theory is inconsistent when it entails a contradiction – i.e., the theory entails both 'p' and 'it is not the case that p' for some sentence 'p'.

Indexical expressions: An indexical expression is a name-like expression, such as 'I', 'you' and 'that', whose referent on a given occasion of use depends in a systematic way on the context in which it is used.

Law of excluded middle: The law of excluded middle is the logical principal according to which 'p or not-p' is true for every sentence 'p'.

Lexical ambiguity: A sentence contains a lexical ambiguity when a word in the sentence has multiple possible interpretations, such as the word 'bank', which can either refer to a type of financial institution or to a type of geographical area.

Material equivalence: The condition that p is materially equivalent to the condition that q when in actual fact, either (i) p and q or (ii) it is not the case that p and it is not the case that q.

Meaning sensitivity: Truth is meaning sensitive if and only if for some sentence 'p', whether 'p' is true depends on the meaning of 'p'.

Model: In formal logic, a model is a logically possible universe.

Necessary condition: The condition that p is a necessary condition for the condition that q when it impossible for it to be the case that q without it also being the case that p.

Necessary equivalence: The condition that p is necessarily equivalent to the condition that q when in every possible world, either (i) p and q or (ii) it is not the case that p and it is not the case that q.

Predicate: A predicate is a linguistic expression, such as 'is taller than', which combines with one or more names to produce a sentence.

Reference magnetism: Reference magnetism is the view that the referent of a predicate is the most natural property or relation which best fits the way we have historically used that predicate.

Relativism: Relativism about truth is the view that sentences are not true absolutely, but rather are only true relative to some other factor. Typically, relativists take the other factor to be something like the way the user of the sentence conceptualizes the world.

Responsiveness: Truth is responsive if and only if for any sentence 'p', whether 'p' is true is determined by whether p, and not the other way around.

Scope ambiguity: A sentence contains a scope ambiguity when the sentence can be interpreted differently depending on how the components of the sentence are grouped together.

Sufficient condition: The condition that p is a sufficient condition for the condition that q when it impossible for it to be the case that p without it also being the case that q.

Theory: A theory is a collection of sentences.

T-schema: The T-schema is the principle that for any sentence 'p', 'p' is true if and only if p.

Truth condition: The truth condition of a sentence is the worldly condition under which, in actual fact, the sentence is true. For an English sentence 'p', the truth condition of 'p' is the condition that p.

Truthmaker: A truthmaker of a sentence is an entity whose existence is responsible for making the sentence true.

Truth supervenes on being: Truth supervenes on being is the thesis that there can be no difference in the state of reality without a difference in which entities exist.

Undecidable statement: The statement 'p' is undecidable when neither 'p' nor 'not-p' is verifiable.

Use-mention distinction: A word is mentioned in a sentence when it occurs surrounding by quotation marks, which results in the word itself being referred to. A word is used in a sentence when it occurs without quotation marks surrounding it, and so refers to something else.

Verification condition: Suppose there is a procedure P and outcome O such that if P is followed and O is obtained then the community of speakers will agree to accept 'p'. The verification condition of 'p' is the condition that following P would result in O.

NOTE ON RELATIVISM

For advanced readers, we more precisely formulate the argument against strong relativism given in Section 1.3.10. Let $Tr(\ulcorner\varphi\urcorner, C)$ assert that φ is true relative to context C and let $Tr(\ulcorner\varphi\urcorner)$ assert that φ is true. We assume the binary truth-in-a-context predicate belongs only to the metalanguage and so can unproblematically be applied to *any* sentence of the object language – including those sentences that contain the monadic truth predicate.

Strong relativism about truth, as defined in Section 1.3.10, is the following thesis:

(Strong Relativism)   There exists a sentence φ such that (i) φ does not contain any truth-related notions, (ii) for all contexts C_1 and C_2,

$$Tr(\ulcorner\varphi\urcorner, C_1) \leftrightarrow Tr(\ulcorner\varphi\urcorner, C_2)$$

and (iii) for some contexts C_1 and C_2,

$$Tr(\ulcorner Tr(\ulcorner\varphi\urcorner)\urcorner, C_1) \wedge \neg Tr(\ulcorner Tr(\ulcorner\varphi\urcorner)\urcorner, C_2).$$

Suppose for a reductio that strong relativism is true. Let φ be the sentence that witnesses strong relativism and let C_1, C_2 be the contexts witnessing condition (iii). When restricted to sentences that do not contain any truth-related notions, the T-schema holds in every context. Consequently, we have by condition (i) that for every context C,

$$Tr(\ulcorner Tr(\ulcorner \varphi \urcorner) \leftrightarrow \varphi \urcorner, C).$$

Thus, for every context C,

$$Tr(\ulcorner Tr(\ulcorner \varphi \urcorner) \urcorner, C) \leftrightarrow Tr(\ulcorner \varphi \urcorner, C).$$

Hence, by condition (iii),

$$Tr(\ulcorner \varphi \urcorner, C_1) \wedge \neg Tr(\ulcorner \varphi \urcorner, C_2).$$

which contradicts condition (ii).

B

NOTE ON CORRESPONDENCE

For advanced readers, we more precisely formulate the analysis of correspondence described in Section 2.1.2.22.1.2. Suppose our language is built from a set of names $\{c_1, c_2, c_3, \ldots\}$ and, for every $n \geq 1$, a set of n-place predicates $\{R_1, R_2, R_3, \ldots\}$. The sentences of our language are defined as follows:

1. If R is an n-place predicate and $c_1, \ldots, c_n$ are names then $R(c_1, \ldots, c_n)$ is a sentence.
2. If φ and ψ are sentences then $(\varphi \vee \psi)$ and $(\varphi \wedge \psi)$ are sentences.
3. If φ is a sentence then $\neg\varphi$ is a sentence.
4. Nothing else is a sentence.

Suppose $\mathcal{O}$ is the set of objects and, for each $n \geq 1$, $\mathcal{R}[n]$ is the set of n-place relations. Each name c has a referent $|c| \in \mathcal{O}$ and each n-place predicate R has a referent $|R| \in \mathcal{R}[n]$.

A *potential* atomic fact is a sequence $\langle \mathbf{R}, a_1, \ldots, a_n \rangle$, where $a_1, \ldots, a_n \in \mathcal{O}$ and $\mathbf{R} \in \mathcal{R}[n]$. We suppose that a primitive incompatibility relation is defined on the set of potential atomic facts, and write $f_1 \perp f_2$ to indicate that f_1 is incompatible with f_2. $\perp$ is required to be symmetric (i.e., if $f_1 \perp f_2$ then $f_2 \perp f_1$).

Some potential atomic facts exist concretely and others do not. Let $\mathcal{A}$ be the set of concretely existing potential atomic facts. We require that $\mathcal{A}$ satisfies the following condition:

(Exclusion) For every potential atomic fact f, $f \notin \mathcal{A}$ if and only if there exists $f' \in \mathcal{A}$ such that $f \perp f'$.

We now identify a concretely existing fact with a non-empty set $\{f_1, \dots, f_n\} \subseteq \mathcal{A}$, which represents the compound fact $f_1 + \cdots + f_n$. We do not distinguish between f and $\{f\}$.

Let $|\varphi|$ denote the set of concretely existing facts to which the sentence φ corresponds. $|\varphi|$ is defined recursively as follows:

1. $|R(c_1, \dots, c_n)| = \begin{cases} \{\langle |R|, |c_1|, \dots, |c_n| \rangle\} & \text{if } \langle |R|, |c_1|, \dots, |c_n| \rangle \in \mathcal{A} \\ \emptyset & \text{otherwise} \end{cases}$
2. $|\neg R(c_1, \dots, c_n)| = \{f \in \mathcal{A} : f \perp \langle |R|, |c_1|, \dots, |c_n| \rangle\}$
3. $|\varphi \vee \psi| = |\varphi| \cup |\psi|$
4. $|\varphi \wedge \psi| = \{\{f_1, \dots, f_n\} \cup \{g_1, \dots, g_m\} : \{f_1, \dots, f_n\} \in |\varphi|, \{g_1, \dots, g_m\} \in |\psi|\}$
5. $|\neg(\varphi \vee \psi)| = |\neg \varphi \wedge \neg \psi|$
6. $|\neg(\varphi \wedge \psi)| = |\neg \varphi \vee \neg \psi|$
7. $|\neg \neg \varphi| = |\varphi|$.

A sentence φ is true if and only if $|\varphi| \neq \emptyset$.

NOTE ON THE SEMANTIC THEORY

It is possible to define semantic correctness in a non-circular manner, using a neat technique first utilized in this context by Alfred Tarski. Let *English⁻* denote the part of English formed by repeatedly applying 'or', 'and', 'not' to atomic sentences free of truth-related vocabulary. The non-circular definition of semantic correctness for English⁻ is as follows:

(Non-Circular)   A sentence of English⁻ is semantically correct when it belongs to the smallest set S such that

    (i) '$t_1,...,t_n$ are R-related' belongs to S if and only if the objects referred to by $t_1, \ldots, t_n$, in that order, stand in the relation referred to by R

    (ii) '$t_1,...,t_n$ are not R-related' belongs to S if and only if the objects referred to by $t_1, \ldots, t_n$, in that order, do not stand in the relation referred to by R

    (iii) if both of 'p', 'q' belong to S then '(p and q)' belongs to S

    (iv) if at least one of 'p', 'q' belongs to S then '(p or q)' belongs to S

    (v) if 'p' belongs to S then 'not not p' belongs to S

(vi) if both of 'not p', 'not q' belong to S then 'not $(p$ or $q)$' belongs to S

(vii) if at least one of 'not p', 'not q' belongs to S then 'not $(p$ and $q)$' belongs to S.

THE INDIRECT LIAR

Let $W(x)$ mean that x is written on the whiteboard, and 'Every $F(x) : \varphi(x)$' mean that everything which satisfies F also satisfies φ. Suppose 'Every $W(x): \neg Tr(x)$' is the only sentence written on the whiteboard. Suppose further that $\mathcal{T}$ contains an adequate theory of truth and is aware of the fact that 'Every $W(x): \neg Tr(x)$' is the only sentence written on the whitboard. Then, we should have

R1. $\mathcal{T} \vDash W(\ulcorner \text{Every } W(x) : \neg Tr(x) \urcorner)$
R2. If $\mathcal{T} \vDash \varphi(\ulcorner \text{Every } W(x) : \neg Tr(x) \urcorner)$ then $\mathcal{T} \vDash \text{Every } W(x) : \varphi(x)$.

To derive a contradiction, we do not require the indiscernability of identicals. Instead, we require the principle of universal elimination (or *UE* for short):

(UE) If $\mathcal{T} \vDash \text{Every } F(x) : \varphi(x)$ and $\mathcal{T} \vDash F(a)$ then $\mathcal{T} \vDash \varphi(a)$.

Universal elimination falls directly out of the meaning of *every* − if it is really true that every F has property φ, and some particular object is an F, then that object has property φ.

Here is the indirect liar derivation:

1. $\mathcal{T} + Tr(\ulcorner \text{Every } W(x) : \neg Tr(x) \urcorner) \vDash Tr(\ulcorner \text{Every } W(x) : \neg Tr(x) \urcorner)$
    [by definition of $\vDash$]

2. $\mathcal{T} + Tr(\ulcorner \text{Every } W(x) : \neg Tr(x)\urcorner) \vDash \text{Every } W(x) : \neg Tr(x)$ [from 1 by T-equivalence]
3. $\mathcal{T} + Tr(\ulcorner \text{Every } W(x) : \neg Tr(x)\urcorner) \vDash \neg Tr(\ulcorner \text{Every } W(x) : \neg Tr(x)\urcorner)$ [frc 2, R1 by UE]
4. $\mathcal{T} \vDash \neg Tr(\ulcorner \text{Every } W(x) : \neg Tr(x)\urcorner)$ [from 3 by reductio]
5. $\mathcal{T} \vDash \text{Every } W(x) : \neg Tr(x)$ [from 4 by R2]
6. $\mathcal{T} \vDash Tr(\ulcorner \text{Every } W(x) : \neg Tr(x)\urcorner)$ [from 5 by T-equivalence].

The contradiction is formed by lines 4 and 6.

A CONDITIONAL FOR TRUTH
THEORIES

E.1 INTRODUCTION

Section 1.3.8 introduced the liar paradox and its effects on an unrestricted T-schema. The truth about liar-like sentences (and other truth-theoretic paradoxes) remains controversial.[36] While there is a lot of work on so-called nonclassical accounts of logical entailment, much of which is directly related to truth-theoretic paradox, our sole aim in this appendix is to give a very simple and somewhat crude example of how nonstandard accounts of conditionals might afford an unrestricted T-schema despite liar or so-called Curry paradox. We aim not to give a full account; we aim only to sketch the general direction.[37]

E.2 T-SCHEMA CONDITIONALS

The T-schema is a biconditional. Biconditionals are just conjunctions of conditionals. Let $\rightarrow$ be the conditional involved in the T-schema, where Tr is the truth predicate, φ is any sentence and $\ulcorner \varphi \urcorner$ is a quotation name of φ:

$$Tr(\ulcorner \varphi \urcorner) \leftrightarrow \varphi =_{df} (Tr(\ulcorner \varphi \urcorner) \to \varphi) \land (\varphi \to Tr(\ulcorner \varphi \urcorner))$$

Features of $\to$ (and conjunction) therefore determine features of $\leftrightarrow$. For present purposes, some features that, depending on its semantics, $\to$ (and, in turn, $\leftrightarrow$) might have are these:

- Detachment: φ together with $\varphi \to \psi$ entails ψ.[38]
- Absorption: $\varphi \to (\varphi \to \psi)$ entails $\varphi \to \psi$.

These features can be described in much more general form but, for present purposes, the given descriptions suffice to convey the basic ideas. What is notable is that these features are not true of all conditionals even though true of the most familiar conditionals.

E.3   LIAR PARADOX AND CURRY'S PARADOX

The liar is just one of many truth-theoretic paradoxes. Of special interest for the T-schema is so-called Curry's paradox. What can be shown (though we do not show it here) is that if the following trio of facts holds for a given conditional and the entailment (or validity or consequence) relation in a given theory, then the theory (closed under such entailment) is the so-called *trivial theory* – which is the theory (or set of sentences) that contains *all* sentences in the language of the theory.

1. T-schema: $Tr(\ulcorner \varphi \urcorner) \leftrightarrow \varphi$.
2. Detachment: φ together with $\varphi \to \psi$ entails ψ.
3. Absorption: $\varphi \to (\varphi \to \psi)$ entails $\varphi \to \psi$.

To see the problem, consider a typical Curry sentence like 'If I'm true then every sentence is true', which can be formally represented as a sentence C which is equivalent to $Tr(\ulcorner C \urcorner) \to \bot$, where $\bot$ is a sentence (like 'every sentence is true') that entails every sentence.[39] The problem then just falls out of the trio of would-be facts above. To begin, the T-schema entails its C instance, namely,

$$Tr(\ulcorner C \urcorner) \leftrightarrow (Tr(\ulcorner C \urcorner) \to \bot)$$

But, now, since the biconditional in the T-schema is just a conjunction of conditionals, each given instance entails both 'directions' of the biconditional;[40] so, in particular, the C instance of the T-schema entails

$$Tr(\ulcorner C \urcorner) \to (Tr(\ulcorner C \urcorner) \to \bot)$$

which, by the assumed Absorption feature, entails

$$Tr(\ulcorner C \urcorner) \to \bot$$

which, by the assumed Detachment feature (going from right to left in the initial C instance of the T-schema), entails

$$Tr(\ulcorner C \urcorner)$$

which, by the assumed Detachment feature again (but this time applied to the preceding line $Tr(\ulcorner C \urcorner) \to \bot$), entails

$$\bot$$

which, as above, entails all sentences in the language of the given theory.

The upshot is that, at least if the logical vocabulary is otherwise standard, no T-schema can have a conditional and entailment relation of which the given trio of facts is true.

E.4 A SIMPLE BUT NONSTANDARD SEMANTICS

Our aim here is merely to sketch a very simple (and in many ways blunt) approach towards a conditional and corresponding entailment relation that avoids satisfying all three features. In particular, the simple goal (without worrying about other desiderata for conditionals) is to find a conditional $\Rightarrow$ and entailment relation $\vDash_*$ such that only the first and second features are validated (by the entailment relation). In short, the goal is to have:

1. T-schema: $Tr(\ulcorner \varphi \urcorner) \Leftrightarrow \varphi$.
2. Detachment: φ together with $\varphi \Rightarrow \psi$ entails, according to $\vDash_*$, ψ.[41]

3. Absorption: $\varphi \Rightarrow (\varphi \Rightarrow \psi)$ does *not* entail, according to $\vDash_*$, $\varphi \Rightarrow \psi$.

The account is one that 'modalises' the semantics for the conditional in a so-called abnormal-worlds fashion.[42]

E.4.1 BASIC SEMANTICS FOR THE CONDITIONAL

Instead of thinking of sentences being true or false at one particular world (e.g., at our actual world), we 'modalise' matters by imagining a nonempty universe W of worlds at each of which all sentences are either true or false (and not both). We can let the purely logical vocabulary (e.g., conjunction, disjunction, negation, usual first-order quantifiers) have their usual truth-at-a-world and falsity-at-a-world conditions. But when it comes to the target conditional $\Rightarrow$, a *difference* among the worlds in W makes a critical difference.

W is in fact the union of two different types of worlds: a nonempty set of normal worlds and a set (possibly empty) of abnormal worlds. As above, at all worlds (normal or abnormal) the purely logical vocabulary behaves the same; they have their usual truth/falsity conditions at all worlds. But when it comes to the target conditional, things are different; the target conditional behaves erratically – indeed, arbitrarily – at abnormal worlds, even if at all normal worlds it has very familiar truth/falsity conditions.

To make the basic idea precise, we give the following truth/falsity conditions for the target conditional (viz., $\Rightarrow$), where, note well, i is an *arbitrary assigner of truth values* at abnormal worlds (i.e., it simply assigns either truth or falsity to sentences in a random way except for logical vocabulary, which it treats normally):

1. Normal worlds: let w be a *normal* world in W. Then
   (a) $A \Rightarrow B$ is true at w iff there is *no* world w' (of any sort) in W such that A is true at w' but B is untrue at w'.
   (b) $A \Rightarrow B$ is false at w otherwise.
2. Abnormal worlds: let w be an *abnormal* world in W.
   (a) $A \Rightarrow B$ is true at w iff arbitrary assigner i assigns truth to $A \Rightarrow B$ at w.
   (b) $A \Rightarrow B$ is false at w iff arbitrary assigner i assigns falsity to $A \Rightarrow B$ at w.

In short, the target conditional has its usual truth/falsity conditions when at normal worlds but otherwise – at abnormal worlds – its truth or falsity turns entirely on random assignment.

E.4.2 ENTAILMENT RELATION

The target entailment relation $\vDash_*$ is defined in the usual 'absence of counterexample' fashion, but a counterexample is restricted to *normal worlds* of a universe $\mathcal{W}$ of worlds.

E.4.2.1 Counterexamples

Let X be a set of sentences and A any sentence. Then a *counterexample* to the pattern $X\therefore A$ is any universe of worlds $\mathcal{W}$ such that there's a *normal world* w at which everything in X is true but A is not true there.

There may be many abnormal worlds at which everything in X is true but A untrue; however, no such abnormal worlds count as counterexamples to $X\therefore A$ even though such abnormal worlds might be essentially involved in a genuine counterexample to the given pattern.

E.4.2.2 Entailment: $\vDash_*$

With the definition of *counterexample* above (viz., Section E.4.2), the definition of entailment is per usual: $X\vDash_* A$ iff there's no counterexample to $X\therefore A$.

In other worlds, X entails, according to $\vDash_*$, the sentence A just if there's no *normal world* of any universe $\mathcal{W}$ whereat everything in X is true but A untrue.

E.5 T-SCHEMA, DETACHMENT, AND ABSORPTION

Taking stock, we now have a conditional (viz., $\Rightarrow$) and entailment relation (viz., $\vDash_*$) of which only the T-schema and detachment may be true; absorption is invalid according to $\vDash_*$. Take each in turn, in reverse order.

E.5.1   ABSORPTION IS INVALID ACCORDING TO $\vDash_*$

The invalidity of Absorption may be seen via a counterexample. Let $\mathcal{W} = \{@, w\}$ wherein $@$ is normal but w is abnormal. Let A be false at $@$ but true at w. Let B be false at w and $@$. (Strictly, B can be true at $@$ without effect on the counterexample.) Finally, let arbitrary assigner i assign *truth* to $A \Rightarrow B$ at the abnormal world w. Now consider the truth and falsity conditions for $\Rightarrow$ sentences, and in particular consider the value of

$$A \Rightarrow (A \Rightarrow B)$$

at the lone normal world $@$ in $\mathcal{W}$. This conditional is true at $@$ iff there's no world in $\mathcal{W}$ at which A is true but $A \Rightarrow B$ untrue. The only world at which A is true is the abnormal world w, but w is also a world in which $A \Rightarrow B$ is true (since the arbitrary evaluator i assigns it truth there). Hence, the value of $A \Rightarrow (A \Rightarrow B)$ at the lone normal world $@$ in $\mathcal{W}$ is *truth*.

So far so good. To get a counterexample to Absorption we need $A \Rightarrow B$ to be *untrue* at the normal world $@$. And we've got that: there is a world in $\mathcal{W}$ at which A is true but B untrue. What world? Answer: w. Yes, w is an abnormal world, but it's still a world in the universe $\mathcal{W}$. Hence, by the normal-worlds falsity conditions, $A \Rightarrow B$ is false at normal world $@$.

Putting everything together: there's a normal world (viz., $@$) in the universe $\mathcal{W}$ at which $A \Rightarrow (A \Rightarrow B)$ is true but $A \Rightarrow B$ untrue. Hence, according to the definition of *counterexample*, there's a counterexample to Absorption. Hence, according to the definition of entailment (viz., $\vDash_*$), Absorption is invalid:

$$\varphi \Rightarrow (\varphi \Rightarrow \psi) \nvDash_* \varphi \Rightarrow \psi.$$

And that's what we needed to show.

E.5.2   DETACHMENT IS VALID ACCORDING TO $\vDash_*$

To show the validity, according to $\vDash_*$, of Detachment we must show that there can be no counterexample to the pattern

$$\varphi, \varphi \Rightarrow \psi \therefore \psi$$

which requires us to show that there can be no *normal* world of a universe W in which both φ and $\varphi \Rightarrow \psi$ are true but ψ untrue.

We can show as much by so-called reductio. Suppose, for reductio (i.e., for a reduction of the assumption to absurdity), that we do have a counterexample to Detachment, and hence that for some universe W there is a normal world @ at which both φ and $\varphi \Rightarrow \psi$ are true but ψ is untrue at @. Since $\varphi \Rightarrow \psi$ is true at the *normal world* @, the truth conditions for $\Rightarrow$ sentences requires that there be *no* world in W – *including* @ *itself* – at which φ is true but ψ is untrue. But this is absurd given the assumption at the start that @ is just such a world at which φ is true and ψ is untrue. Hence, our initial assumption must be rejected; there can be no counterexample to Detachment.

E.5.3   T-SCHEMA AND CURRY SENTENCES

Given that $\Rightarrow$ satisfies Detachment but not Absorption, at least under the given entailment relation (viz., $\vDash_*$), the conditional is a candidate for use in the T-schema despite the existence of Curry sentences. Without Absorption, the Curry derivation in Section E.3 is invalid.

The invalidity of the Curry derivation doesn't alone resolve all concerns about Curry's paradox or, generally, truth-theoretic paradoxes. But at least the reader can see that the hope of an unrestricted T-schema for truth is not in vain.

E.6   NONCLASSICAL LOGIC

Other options for responding to truth-theoretic paradox involve not only (if at all) a nonstandard semantics for conditionals but instead (or, perhaps, also) a nonstandard account of logical entailment itself. Some details of how this account might go are given in Chapter 7 of this book. Interested readers might also consult *Logic: The Basics* (Routledge: New York, 2017) for a gentle and user-friendly introduction to both the standard account of logical entailment and representative nonstandard (so-called subclassical) accounts of logical entailment, accounts that are directly related to truth-theoretic paradox.

NOTES

36. In *Formal Theories of Truth* (Oxford University Press: Oxford, 2018) Beall, Glanzberg and Ripley introduce representative accounts of truth and paradox.

37. And we do not prove that the account can 'work' in the technical sense of a target theory's having a model. That task depends on much more than just the semantics of the target theory's conditional.

38. Throughout, the entailment relation might be the foundational one (viz., logical) or some extra-logical entailment relation governing some would-be true theory. (To be logical entailment, all vocabulary in the would-be logically valid form must be logical vocabulary.)

39. If you want to think about how such a sentence might arise in ordinary language, just imagine a name 'c' being given for the sentence 'If c is true then every sentence is true'. In short, c *just is* the sentence 'If c is true then every sentence is true'.

40. In other words, $A \leftrightarrow B$ is logically equivalent to $(A \rightarrow B) \wedge (B \rightarrow A)$, which logically entails $A \rightarrow B$ and also $B \rightarrow A$, since every logical conjunction $C \wedge D$ logically entails both 'conjuncts' (i.e., the C and D parts).

41. In what follows we write this, per standard practice, as $\varphi, \varphi \Rightarrow \psi \vDash_* \psi$.

42. For but some of the work along these lines see any of Jc Beall, *Spandrels of Truth* (Oxford University Press: Oxford, 2009); Hartry Field, *Saving Truth from Paradox* (Oxford University Press: Oxford, 2008); and Graham Priest, *In Contradiction* (Clarendon Press: Oxford, 1987).

INDEX

Printed in the United States
by Baker & Taylor Publisher Services